T0351260

China's Urban Labor Market

To my parents

China's Urban Labor Market

A Structural Econometric Approach

Yang Liu

Kyoto University Press

香港大學出版社
HONG KONG UNIVERSITY PRESS

The publication of this book was supported by a President's Discretionary Budget of Kyoto University for Young Scholar's Research Results.

Kyoto University Press
Yoshida South Campus
Kyoto University
69 Konoe-cho Yoshida
Sakyo, Kyoto 606-8315
Japan
www.kyoto-up.or.jp
ISBN 978-4-87698-285-1 *(Hardback)*

Hong Kong University Press
The University of Hong Kong
Pokfulam Road
Hong Kong
www.hkupress.org
ISBN 978-988-8208-04-3 *(Hardback)*

British Library Cataloguing-in-Publication Data
A catalogue record for this book is available from the British Library.

10　9　8　7　6　5　4　3　2　1

Printed and bound by Fish Eye Co., Hong Kong, China

Contents

List of Tables

List of Figures

Preface

For a long time, China's labor market has been considered to be a special case, because of the degree of influence left over from the country's previous planned economy. Since the economic revolution and enterprise reforms of the 1990s, however, the labor market in China has shared an increasing number of common characteristics with market-driven economies, such as firms' profit maximization, market competition, and optimal behavior of workers. Against the background of such changes in the labor market of the country, our study adopts a new approach to examine the Chinese context, namely the use of structural econometric models based on modern economics to examine contemporary issues in the labor market of urban China.

Up till the 1970s, jobs and workers in China were controlled under the planned economy, in which the national government dictated employment and wage levels. The economic revolution started in 1978 transformed China from a planned economy to a market-driven economy, in which workers were free to search for jobs and firms were free to recruit suitable workers. The first job agency started its business in 1980, and by the end of the 1980s, over 20,000 job agencies across China were providing job-search and recruitment services for workers and firms. Building on this development, the reform of state-owned enterprises in the 1990s exposed millions of urban workers that had previously been under the protection of the government to a competitive job market. While most of the workers from the state-owned sector faced unemployment, firms enjoyed the freedom to pursue profit maximization and thus a more dynamic labor market was formed. Although accompanied by many unsolved problems, such as strict government control and imperfect information, China has made great strides towards a real labor market.

In the light of the foregoing, our study employs structural econometric models in order to examine the issues of disequilibrium of labor supply and demand, impact of rural–urban migration on the urban labor market, job creation and destruction, labor market matching, and the Beveridge curve. The selection of these issues was driven by the motivation to find out the economic reasons behind the high unemployment rate in China, which has remained a puzzle despite the country's rapid economic growth.

To tackle these issues, the structure of this book follows an economic theoretical framework. We begin from the approach of labor supply and demand theory in Part 1. In Part II, we proceed the study into the framework of search and matching theory, which is one of the most popular theories in modern labor economics, though it has not captured the attention of scholars of the Chinese labor market.

Our study could be the first one to use structural econometric models to examine China's urban labor market. A reviewer of this book has commented that "it is distinctive for its formal theoretical modeling and structural estimation approach, which is different from previous researches on the topic that I have seen. A lot of appreciation of such rigorous treatment of empirical questions has been expressed." Thus, I hope it not only provides insights into China's labor market, but also serves as a basis for applying modern structural econometric models to analyze this issue in the future.

In completing this book, I have received generous support from many people and institutes. I would like to express my heartfelt gratitude to Professor Kenn Ariga at the Institute of Economic Research, Kyoto University, for his valuable comments and suggestions throughout this study. I am also grateful to the anonymous referees, Prof. Fumio Ohtake, Prof. Masaru Sasaki, Prof. Deqiang Liu, Prof. Daiji Kawaguchi, Prof. Hiroshi Ohnishi, Prof. Go Yano, Prof. Ayako Kondo, Prof. Yoshihisa Inada, Prof. Toshihiko Hayashi, Prof. Ryoichi Imai, Prof. Hiroaki Miyamoto, Prof. Takatoshi Tsukamoto, Prof. Konstantinos Eleftheriou, Prof. Patrick Puhani, and Prof. Dmitriy Krichevskiy, for their useful comments.

I would also like to express my thanks to the generous funding provided by the Institutional Program for Young Researcher Overseas

Visits and Asian CORE Program, Japan Society for the Promotion of Science, which allowed me to attend several international conferences and exchange ideas with scholars around the world. These interactions certainly helped improve our study.

I am grateful to the Asia Pacific Institute of Research as well as the Graduate School of Economics at Kyoto University, and all my colleagues there, for their great help in completing our study. Thanks are also due to Kyoto University Press and Hong Kong University Press for undertaking the publication of this book and their hard work in the publishing process. I deeply acknowledge the *Soutyou Sairyou Keihi* Discretionary Fund from Kyoto University for supporting the preparation of the final manuscripts and publication. I would also like to thank Dr. Mitsuhiro Okano and Dr. Mingxiu Zhao for their generous help with editing the figures in this book, and Editage for providing editorial assistance.

Last but not least, I wish to thank the editors and copyright holders of the following journals for granting me permission to use the materials that I first published through them: *China Economic Review* © Elsevier Inc., *Hitotsubashi Journal of Economics* © Hitotsubashi University, *The Chinese Economy* © M.E. Sharpe, *Tokeigaku (Statistics)* © the Japan Society of Economic Statistics, and *Economics Bulletin* (http://www.economicsbulletin.com/).

Introduction

1

Purpose, Issues, and Outline of the Study

1.1 Purpose and Issues

In the past two decades, China's urban labor market has experienced a rapidly expanding size, dynamic job creation and destruction, and large-scale rural–urban migration. The market economy, which has gradually developed in the country since the early 1980s, has made great progress in its transition towards a real labor market. However, unlike the experiences in a number of other countries, China's rapidly growing urban GDP was continuously accompanied by a high unemployment rate during this period. Understanding the real reason for urban unemployment, against this background of rural–urban migration and structural changes in the urban labor market, has therefore become one of the most important issues for labor market studies in China.

Traditional analyses of China's unemployment have typically focused on the issues of labor demand and supply. However, dramatic job and worker reallocations owing to the economic transition in China have created considerable frictions in the labor market, making the issue of unemployment more complicated than a mere gap between demand and supply (although this imbalance still has an influence). Search and matching theory (e.g. McCall 1970; Mortensen 1986; Mortensen and Pissarides 1999), which takes into account market frictions and imperfect information, has been the most popular approach in labor market analysis in recent years, but little empirical work has been conducted on issues in China. We aim to fill this gap in our study, starting from the conventional labor supply and demand approach to study unemployment, and then proceeding to examine the issue of unemployment in China using the search and matching approach.

In spite of the country's rapid economic growth and active job creation, urban unemployment remains high in China,[1] and this remains an obstacle to attempts to reduce poverty and earnings differentials. Therefore, labor market development and unemployment control have become important issues for China.

On the basis of the foregoing, the present study aims to answer the following three research questions:

1. Why does labor supply exceed labor demand for urban residents in China?
2. Does rural–urban migration reduce labor demand for urban residents?
3. Why has unemployment coexisted with a shortage of workers over recent years?

Although an imbalance between labor supply and demand in China has been identified in previous studies, its causes remain unclear, and little effort has been made to examine this phenomenon in the light of economic theories. To understand the real reasons for such imbalance, we apply traditional economic theories. Classical economic theories suggest that ongoing equilibrium between supply and demand in a Walrasian labor market would be achieved through permanent adjustment of real wages, so that there would be no unemployment (Romer 2005). However, in the short and medium run, disequilibrium in supply and demand often exists. This disequilibrium arises from a certain rigidity that hinders permanent adjustment in the labor market, as suggested by Keynesian economists (see Cahuc and Zylberberg 2004), and is the fundamental reason for the imbalance between the labor supply and demand for urban residents in China.

Furthermore, an imbalance can also result from a shift in the labor demand curve of urban residents, which is caused by changes in the prices of other factors and output levels under a conditional demand framework. Therefore, against the background of large-scale rural–urban migration, these changes in China could have been caused by the considerable degree of migration over the past two decades. This issue brings forward the second research question of this book: Does rural–urban migration reduce

---

1. Although the official unemployment rate reported by the government (i.e., the "registered unemployment rate") was around 3–4% in the late 1990s and 2000s, there is a common belief that the real unemployment rate is much higher.

labor demand for urban residents? The few previous empirical studies on this topic have typically used reduced-form approaches that have regressed possible factors, leading to contrasting results. As a result, we construct a structural model for this purpose so as to provide a more complete and in-depth analysis of the mechanisms of wages, production, and labor supply and demand suggested by labor economic theories.

While the first two research questions above can be answered within a labor supply and demand framework, the conflicts revealed by the third question mean it can no longer be explained by traditional theories. In this book, we employ the novel approach of search and matching theory to tackle this issue, which provides a theoretical base for modern unemployment analysis. Imperfect information usually exists in the actual labor market, implying that it takes time for workers to find acceptable jobs and for firms to approach suitable workers. Thus, unemployment is determined not only by the numbers of jobseekers and job vacancies, but also by the search and matching process between them. Search theory provides a modeling framework for that and examines unemployment growth by looking into flows in and out of unemployment. Outflows mainly refer to the reduction of unemployment through new hires from unemployed workers based on job–worker matching and job creation, whereas inflows refer to addition to unemployment mainly through job destruction. Unlike classical and Keynesian theories, this approach can tackle directly the puzzle of the coexistence of high unemployment and high job vacancies in China.

As a result, we design this study of China's urban labor market by examining labor supply and demand, rural–urban immigration, job creation and destruction, and labor market matching, all of which are related to the core item of unemployment determinants in urban China.

1.2   General Theoretical Background

In this study, we adopt two approaches to examine our three research questions. The traditional approach of classical theory and Keynesian theory concentrates on the balances between labor supply and demand; the search-theoretic approach addresses imperfect information and models the job–worker matching process in the dynamic analysis of unemployment evolution.

1.2.1 The Labor Supply and Demand Approach to Unemployment

Under this approach, unemployment arises when the supply of labor exceeds the demand for labor. If the labor market is in perfect competition and has perfect information, wages will bring about a permanent equilibrium between labor supply and labor demand. Under this approach, as shown in Fig. 1.1, the current wage is flexible and always equals the equilibrium wage, W^*. However, from the perspective of Keynesian economics, the current wage, W, can be rigid and fail to react to the supply and demand of labor. Hence, labor supply exceeds labor demand and unemployment, U, is created (Mankiw 2000).

Fig. 1.1 The labor supply and demand approach to unemployment

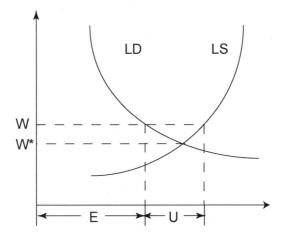

As Keynesian economics can provide explanations of the key determinants of unemployment in such a labor supply and demand framework, this enables us to understand some of the possible causes of unemployment, such as the minimum wage policy, inflation, and wage bargaining by unions.

1.2.2 Search and Matching Theory

In a labor market, jobseekers usually take time to apply for acceptable positions, while firms incur expenses in selecting suitable workers. Hence, unlike classical labor supply and demand theories that assume perfect information, search and matching theory takes into account the fact that imperfect information and frictions are prevalent in the labor market.

This simple introduction to search and matching theory is based on Chapter 1 in Pissarides (2000). Assume that only unemployed workers search for jobs. In a decentralized economy, firms and unemployed workers search and trade in the labor market, and they gradually become matched to each other according to the prevailing matching technology. Now, let us assume that U denotes the number of unemployed workers, V the number of job vacancies, M the number of matches, and a the matching technology (also called matching efficiency). The number of job matches is thus given by a matching function, which we assume for analytical simplicity to be in a Cobb–Douglas form with a constant return to scale, as follows:

$$M = aU^{\eta}V^{1-\eta},$$ (1.1)

where η represents elasticity and $0 < \eta < 1$. This equation of M therefore provides the outflow from employment.

Inflow into unemployment results from job destruction, the rate of which is denoted by λ. Accordingly, the evolution of mean unemployment is given by the difference between the inflow into and outflow from employment, as follows:

$$\dot{U} = \lambda(L - U) - aU^{\eta}V^{1-\eta},$$ (1.2)

where L represents the total labor force. Therefore, in a comparative static analysis, the growth in unemployment will increase if there are reasons to increase the level of λ, and will decrease if a or V are increased owing to related factors.

In the steady state, $\dot{U} = 0$. We define that $\theta \equiv V / U$, which is a measure of market tightness. The rate of change in the state of job vacancies, M / V, is thus obtained as a function of θ, and we define it as $M / V = q(\theta)$. As a result, we obtain the following relationship between U and V:

$$U = \frac{\lambda L}{\lambda + \theta q(\theta)} \quad (\text{where } \theta \equiv V / U).$$ (1.3)

This is the functional form of the Beveridge curve (BC), which is convex to the origin in the space of V and U. A shift in BC reflects structural changes in the labor market, such as a matching technology change, growth in the labor force, or job destruction shock (the details of which are discussed in Chapter 8).

There is another relationship between U and V, as indicated by the job creation condition. The rate of job creation to a given number of jobseekers is $\theta \equiv V / U$. θ is determined by firm behavior, and it indicates the number of jobs created in response to the number of jobseekers in the labor market. Note that if the number of jobseekers increases, firms would create more jobs due to profit maximization, and thus θ is not influenced by changes in the number of jobseekers. Within the space of V and U, the job creation curve (JC) is a line through the origin with the slope θ. JC shifts along with changes in the slope θ, which are determined by factors related to production, such as productivity, interest rates and hiring costs.

BC and JC are manifested in Figs. 1.2 and 1.3. Fig. 1.2 shows the situation in which BC shifts outward. If, for instance, the job–worker matching efficiency declines, more time would be required for jobseekers to apply for acceptable positions and for firms to select suitable workers; thus, both unemployment and job vacancies would increase, moving the equilibrium from E to E'. Fig. 1.3 shows the situation in which an increase in job creation, θ, (which could be due to productivity growth, a cut in interest rates, etc.) shifts JC counterclockwise. In this case, unemployment decreases, job vacancies increase, and the equilibrium moves from E to E''.

Fig. 1.2 BC and JC: the case in which BC shifts

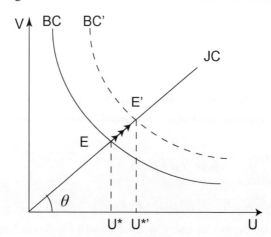

Fig. 1.3 BC and JC: the case in which JC shifts

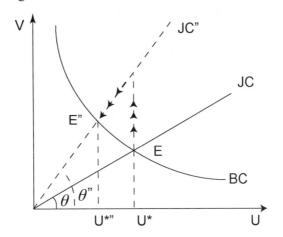

1.3 Outline of the Study

The design of our study is manifested in the structure of this book. Part I deals with the conventional approach of labor supply and demand in studies of China's labor market. We provide an overview of China's urban labor market in Chapter 2 and focus on the labor market for urban residents in Chapter 3, specifically the disequilibrium unemployment of these residents. We then extend this classical approach to the entire urban labor market in Chapter 4 and examine whether rural–urban migration reduces the labor demand for urban residents based on dual labor market theory, conditional and unconditional factor demand, and the product market. Our model identifies two opposite effects of rural–urban migration: a negative effect of substitution and a positive effect on job creation. The comparable size of these two opposite sub-effects is obtained by a static simulation, and finally, we assess how migration as a whole influences the labor demand for urban residents.

Part II deals with our adoption of the search-theoretic approach to examine the effect of frictions and imperfect information on China's labor market. In Chapter 5, we shed light on job rotation and worker reallocation in urban China by assessing job creation, job destruction, as well as worker inflows and outflows. In Chapter 6, we estimate the matching functions of jobs and workers, quantifying the efficiencies of job–worker matching in the labor market. Further, as an important factor that determines the outcome of matches, we examine job creation in Chapter 7, highlighting its specific determinants in China. Finally, the issues of labor market matching, job creation, job destruction, rural–urban migration, and on-the-job searches are combined in the unemployment evolution model, which is presented in Chapter 8. The proposed model allows us to clarify the mechanism of urban unemployment and the relationships among various factors. We conclude the study with perspectives on the development of China's urban labor market.

2

China's Urban Labor Market: An Overview

This chapter sheds light on the situation of China's urban labor market, which is an important background feature of our model. Accompanying economic development and urbanization, the scale of urban employment greatly increased over the past decade[1] owing to rapid population growth and large-scale rural–urban migration. Figs. 2.1 and 2.2 show that the overall employment and population in urban areas in China were more than doubled during the period 1990–2010. Further, rural migrants comprised a growing proportion of all new hires, as shown in Fig. 3.3, which reports annual new hires in terms of *urban units* (*danwei* in Chinese).[2]

One of the most pressing problems in China's urban labor market is unemployment. Since the official unemployment rate presented by the government has long been questionable, we first adjust the formal unemployment rates of 29 provinces[3] in the period 1992–2010 in order to clarify China's real unemployment situation. Given the greatly increasing rural–urban migrant labor force, we then examine the inflows of rural migrant workers, highlighting their characteristics in the labor market. The heterogeneity of migrant and resident workers indicates a dual labor market within the city: a labor market for urban residents and a labor market for rural migrants. Furthermore, there are also vast worker flows within cities, as a result of large-scale economic restructuring, which we examine in the fourth section. Finally, we assess the important role of job agencies in China's labor market.

---

1. No exact data on the labor force in China are available.
2. Most Chinese statistics refer to *urban units*, which include all state-owned enterprises (SOEs), collective enterprises, foreign enterprises, and large and medium-sized private enterprises, while most self-employed businesses and small private enterprises are excluded (NBS 1993–2010a).
3. Hong Kong, Macao, Tibet, Xinjiang and Taiwan are excluded because of data constraints. The 29 provinces are the provincial-level administrative regions, including Beijing, Shanghai, Tianjin, Chongqing, etc. In this book, all provincial-level analyses refer to these 29 provinces.

Fig. 2.1 Urban employment in China over the past two decades

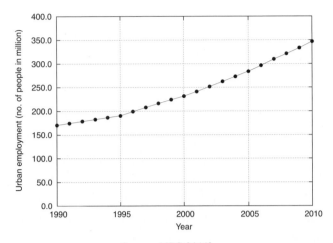

Source: NBS 2011b

Notes:
(1) These data refer to workers who work in urban areas, regardless of whether they have a local household registration (*Hukou* in Chinese) (NBS 2011b).
(2) These national-level statistics cover employment in *urban units*, and also self-employment and employment in other small and informal enterprises.

Fig. 2.2 Chinese population over the past two decades

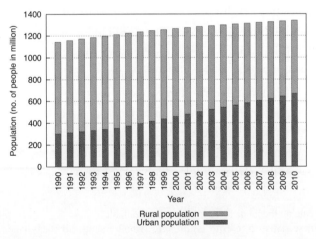

Source: NBS (2011b)

Fig. 2.3 Annual urban new hires from urban residents and rural migrants

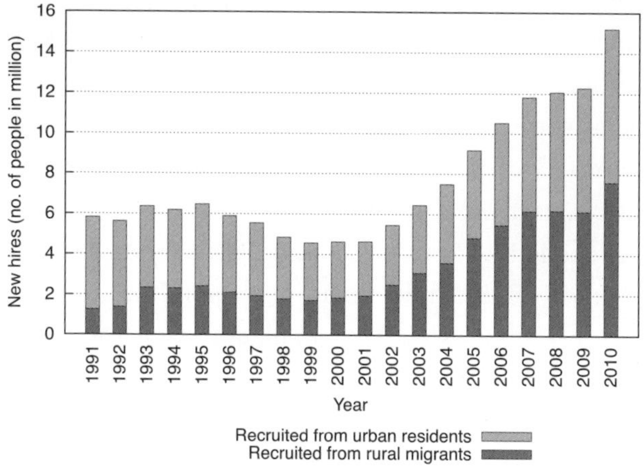

Source: NBS (1992–2011a)

Note: These data refer to new hires in *urban units* and thus exclude self-employment and workers in small or informal private enterprises.

2.1   How High is China's Real Unemployment Rate?

2.1.1 Official Unemployment Rate and the Real Situation

Even though China is in the midst of an unprecedented economic boom, the country's urban unemployment rate remains high. In 2006, the official unemployment rate was 4.1%, but the real situation could be much more serious. For example, if the 11.8 million retrenched workers (NBS 2007a) excluded from the official unemployment statistics were taken into account, the figure would increase to 9.8%. Urban unemployment is therefore one of the most serious problems in China.

Retrenched workers are those that are in a contract of employment but do not currently work, such as workers who have been laid-off or forced to retire early. Retrenched workers are a product of the planned economy, in which the government posted workers to jobs but the system was marred by low economic efficiency. The government has been tackling this problem since the economic revolution in 1978. The enterprise reform initiated in 1986 was fully implemented in the mid-1990s. However, being cushioned by the planned economy, most of the retrenched workers had difficulties in finding new jobs and millions remained unemployed (Knight and Song 2005).

A further problem is that the definitions of unemployment in the population census are often imprecise.[4] Previous studies have adjusted national-level unemployment rates based on regional unemployment surveys and official population data. For example, Knight and Xie (2006) used the official statistics as well as a household sample survey dataset (concerned with 13 cities in six provinces) to estimate national-level unemployment rates from 1993 to 2002 and showed that the figures in urban areas exceeded 11% in 1999 and 2000. Giles et al. (2005) also adjusted national-level unemployment rates using the results of an urban labor survey in five cities as well as population data from China's census, and achieved the real figures of 10%. The findings of these studies suggest that adjusted unemployment rates are much higher than official rates at the national level. Consequently, at the provincial level, it is also important to highlight the real situation of regional unemployment before examining its determinants. In the next section, we thus examine the regional unemployment rate and provide a panel dataset for the adjusted unemployment rate based on a cross-section of 29 provinces and time series of 19 years.

2.1.2 Adjustment for the Provincial-Level Urban Unemployment Rate

In China, the urban unemployment rate is officially referred to as the *urban registered unemployment rate*. This rate is based on the data in the official registers pertaining to urban unemployment (i.e., the local bureaus of labor and social security). It is defined as follows:

$$\text{Urban registered unemployment rate} = \frac{\text{Number of registered urban unemployed residents}}{\text{Total labor force of urban residents}} \times 100\%. \tag{2.1}$$

However, this figure excludes those unemployed workers who have not registered themselves as unemployed. According to Chinese Local Unemployment Registration Regulations, a retrenched worker cannot register if he or she does not possess proof of the contract termination. The

---

4. See Knight and Xie (2006).

unregistered population thus includes the millions of retrenched workers discussed earlier. Although no publicly available data on the number of retrenched workers are available, a World Bank report (1993) stated that 25% of employees in Chinese SOEs in the early 1990s were considered to be surplus labor (see also Knight and Song 2005).

Provincial-level data on retrenched workers for this study were provided by NBS (1993–2011a).[5] Of the 29 studied provinces, Heilongjiang and Liaoning have the largest numbers of retrenched workers, while the numbers in Zhejiang, Fujian and Guangdong are comparatively low. Heilongjiang and Liaoning are bases of heavy industry and house many large state-owned and collective firms, whereas Zhejiang, Fujian and Guangdong, which lie in eastern and southeastern China, have been wrestling with the issues of reform and openness since 1978.

We adjusted the unemployment rate using year-end data for retrenched workers and registered unemployed persons in the following manner:

$$UR_{it}^{ad} = \frac{U^{\text{Reg}}{}_{it} + U^{\text{Ret}}{}_{it}}{LPO_{it}^{\text{Res}}} \times 100\%, \tag{2.2}$$

$$t = 1992, \ldots, 2010 \ (year)$$

where t represents the time series 1992–2010, i the 29 provinces, UR_{it}^{ad} the adjusted unemployment rate for urban residents, and $U^{\text{Reg}}{}_{it}$ and $U^{\text{Ret}}{}_{it}$ the numbers of registered unemployed residents and retrenched workers at the end of year t respectively. (Note that $U^{\text{Ret}}{}_{it}$ excludes the retrenched workers re-employed at time t.) LPO_{it}^{Res} is the total number of urban residents in the labor market (excluding migrants).

Since there are no accurate data on the provincial-level urban labor population, LPO_{it}^{Res} is estimated as follows:

$$LPO_{it}^{\text{Res}} = \frac{U_{it}^{\text{Reg}}}{UR_{it}^{\text{Reg}}}, \tag{2.3}$$

where UR_{it}^{Reg} is the registered unemployment rate for urban residents.

---

5. In this dataset, retrenched workers until 1997 are called *Fuyurenyuan* (surplus workers) and those afterwards *Buzaigangzhigong* (non-posted workers). This category includes workers who have been laid off and currently do not work, but excludes those who have been re-employed.

This adjustment enables us to derive a closer estimation of the real unemployment situation in China (see Fig 2.4). In most provinces, the adjusted rates started increasing in 1994 and peaked in 2000 before declining gradually. By contrast, the registered unemployment rates increased continuously during this period at the national level and the provincial level (except the provinces of Gansu, Qinghai, Yunnan, and Guizhou in western China, which had unusually large numbers of registered unemployed workers in 1994–1997) (Fig. 2.5).

Fig. 2.4 Adjusted unemployment rates

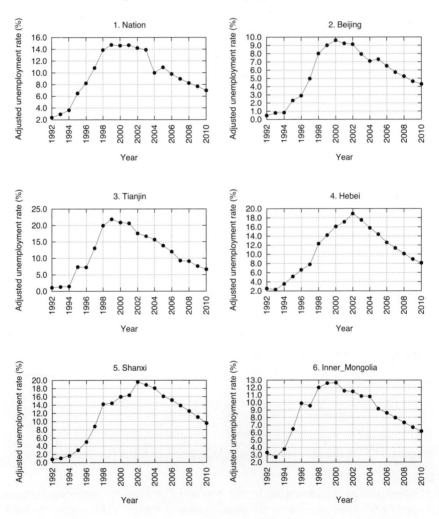

Fig. 2.4 (continued)

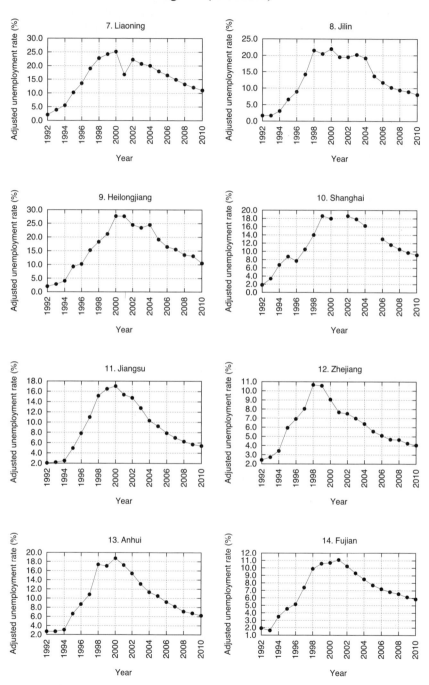

Fig. 2.4 (continued)

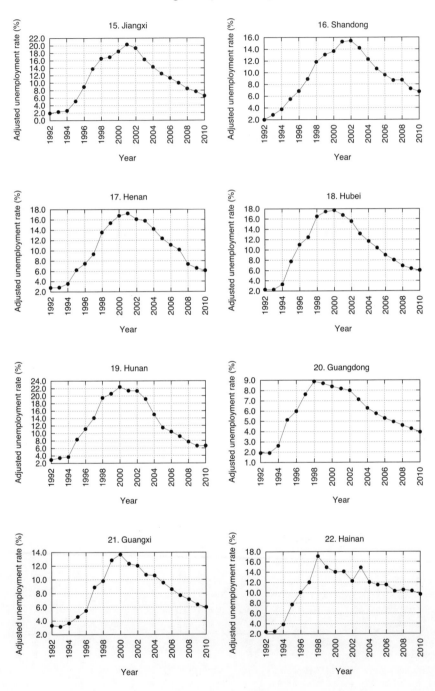

Fig. 2.4 (continued)

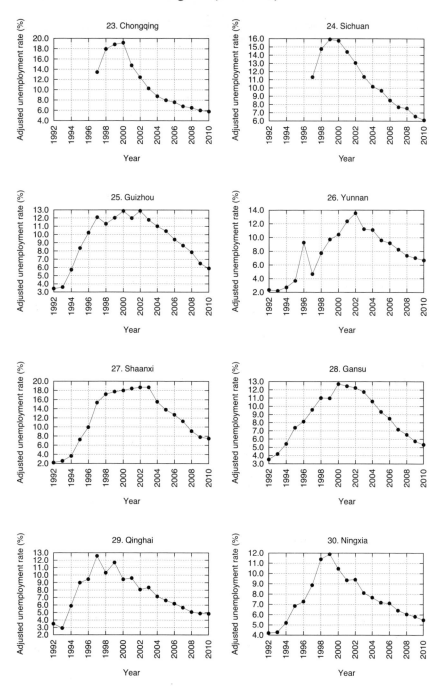

Note: The rates for Sichuan and Chongqing before 1997 were not reported because
Chongqing was part of Sichuan at that time.

Fig. 2.5 Registered unemployment rates

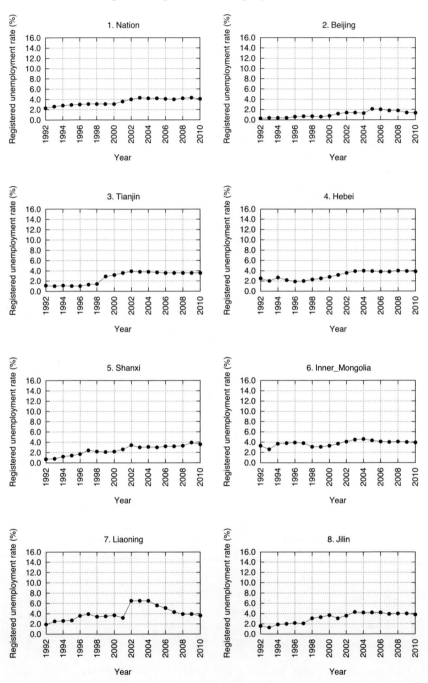

Fig. 2.5 (continued)

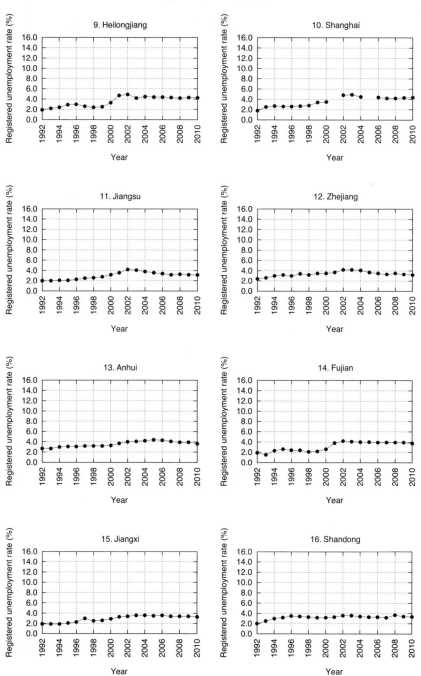

Fig. 2.5 (continued)

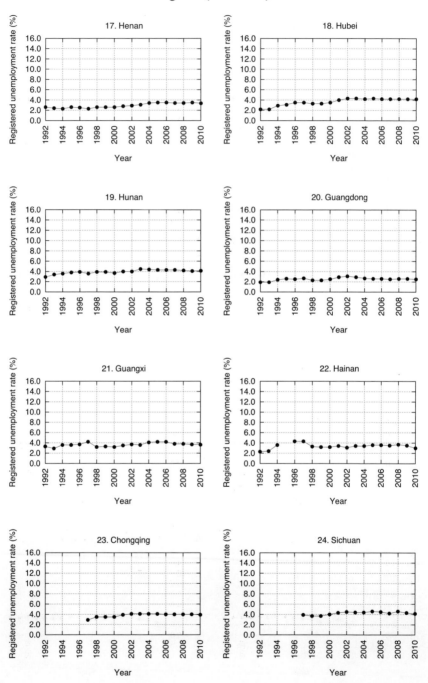

Fig. 2.5 (continued)

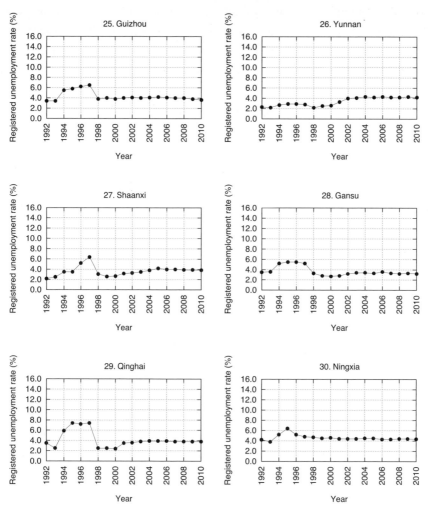

Note: Data derived from the *China Statistical Yearbook 1993–2011*.

The changes observed in the adjusted unemployment rate were concurrent with the process of China's economic revolution. The most effective policies pertaining to the reform of SOEs were implemented in 1993, which were soon followed by the implementation of China's *Company Law*. The economic reform that started in 1994 was accompanied by a rapidly developing market economy; however, this stage was also characterized by redundancies that led to millions of unemployment. From 1997 to 2000, most state-owned and collective enterprises experienced full effects of this reform and the accumulated number of redundant workers peaked. Although the number of surplus workers was declining throughout the 2000s, the decrease was slow, and the adjusted unemployment rate in 2010 was still as high as 7%. Thus, the causes of the unemployment problem could include not only the worker retrenchment project but also other factors, which will be discussed in depth in this book.

Further, as shown in Fig. 2.6, the histograms of both registered and adjusted unemployment rates studied are basically normal distributions. The registered rates range from 0% to 8%, while our adjusted rates range from 0% to 28%. Also, the mean, median and maximum values of the adjusted unemployment rates are approximately three times those of the registered rates.

It is not surprising that the adjusted unemployment rates in some regions were as high as 20%. Indeed, by the end of 2006, the gross accumulated number of retrenched workers across China had exceeded 40 million, approximately 30% of the urban labor force in 1992 (NBS 1993–2007a). Further, our national-level adjusted unemployment rate in 2002 (14.2%) was similar to the 2002 estimate by Giles et al. (2005), namely 14%. Unavoidably, a number of factors may influence the calculation. For instance, some unemployed people might not register at a government office, while some retrenched workers could have found part-time jobs in addition to receiving livelihood subsides from their original companies. Nevertheless, our adjustment certainly reveals the real unemployment situation in China more accurately than the official statistics.

In addition, there are also rural migrants in urban areas, which will be discussed in detail in Section 2.2. These workers migrate to cities for higher incomes, but do not lose their rights in land use and farm work in their areas of origin. Rural migrants are thus not recognized in official urban unemployment figures and are not protected by unemployment insurance if they lose their jobs in the city.[6] As rural migrants have the option of returning to farm work should they lose their urban jobs, they are not included in the scope of unemployment in our study.

---

6. This was the situation in our sample period of 1991–2011. Starting from 2011, rural migrants have been allowed to join the unemployment insurance schemes in some cities.

Fig. 2.6 Provincial-level samples of the studied unemployment rates
(a) Registered unemployment rates (%)

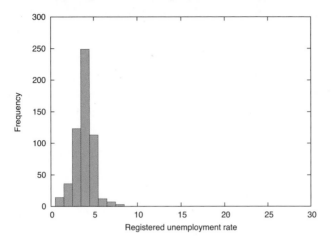

Source: NBS (1993–2011a)

(b) Adjusted unemployment rates (%)

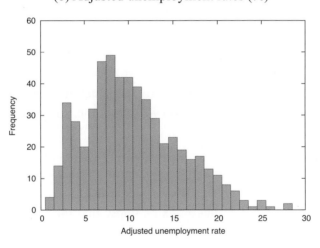

Source: Author's estimation

2.2   Rural Migrant Workers in Urban Areas

China's rural–urban migration has led to a large number of migrant laborers (*nongmingong* in Chinese) in urban areas since the introduction of rural-urban migration in the mid-1980s. A national household survey in 2010 reported that there were 108.9 million, 117.9 million, 132.3 million and 146.9 million rural–urban migrant workers in China in 2003, 2005, 2007 and 2009, respectively (Cai et al. 2010).

Rural migrant workers leave their rural homes in search of temporary jobs in urban areas. They primarily include those who were originally engaged in farm work in rural areas, as well as those who are newly graduates from rural schools. A survey by the central bank of China[7] (Cai et al. 2010) found that, in 2009, 59.3% of the rural labor force had moved to urban areas to take up temporary jobs.[8] Furthermore, the ratio of workers who migrated with their families is increasing, but only one-fifth of this kind of new migrant workers have family members working or studying in the city (Cai et al. 2010).

Among all rural–urban migrants, more than half originated from central and western China. For example, in 2008, 57% of rural migrants originated from the central and western regions of China, compared with 43% with origins in the eastern regions (data from Cai et al. 2010). Furthermore, rural migrants with origins in eastern China typically move within their home provinces. For example, in 2008, almost 80% of migrants with origins in eastern China moved to cities within their home provinces. By contrast, the majority of rural migrants with origins in central and western China (71% from central regions and 63% from western regions) moved to other provinces. The destinations of such inter-provincial migration are generally along the eastern coast of China, including regions such as Guangdong, Zhejiang and Shanghai. These statistics come from the Rural Survey of the China's National Bureau of Statistics (Cai et al. 2010).

The general determinants for migration include income disparity, gender, education level, age, marriage status and land allocation (Zhao 2005; Knight and Song 2005; Bodvarsson and Hou 2010; Xing 2010). Although such migration determinants imply that the human capital of rural–urban migrants is higher than that of most other rural residents, such migrants still have low education levels and skills (Cai et al. 2010). For instance, 83.3% of the rural migrant workers have an education below

---

7. Statistics and Analysis Department, the People's Bank of China.
8. In this survey, the sampling covered 4405 rural households in nine provinces. Of the 11,790 workers questioned, 7001 (59.4%) had left rural homes and worked as *nongmingong* in urban areas.

junior middle school level (NBS 2006d). A survey of six large cities in 1999 and 2000[9] also reported that the number of years of education and work experience of the migrants was much lower than that of urban residents. Education quality and skill training in rural areas have long been behind those in urban areas. Furthermore, most rural migrants are young. For instance, the national survey reported that, in 2009, 61.6% of them were below the age of 30 and 83.9% were below 40 (Cai et al. 2010). Also, many of them are used to physical work and tend to work harder than urban residents (Zhao 2009; ROSC 2006).

These characteristics provide evidence of the heterogeneity of migrant and resident workers in China. However, the most important reason for this heterogeneity is the discrimination arisen from the household registration system (*Hukou*) (Xu 2006; Liu, Yi 2010; Sun and Fan 2011). Public benefits, access to good quality housing, schools and health care, and also attractive employment opportunities are available only to those who have urban household registration (Bao et al. 2009). Furthermore, urban governments protect registered residents by providing them with social insurance and unemployment benefits. By contrast, there is little government protection for migrants. As rural migrants do not have permanent urban household registration, they often receive lower wages for the same work and do not have unions to negotiate wage increases (Meng 2010). For instance, in 2005, the average per-capita wage for rural migrants was 10,332 *yuan*, approximately 60% of the average per-capita wage for urban residents (NBS 2006d). Furthermore, they can neither permanently reside in cities nor enjoy social insurance like official residents (Rupelle et al. 2009; Lin and Zhang 2011); and in particular, they do not receive unemployment benefits, which are limited to urban residents. Moreover, jobless rural migrants are not recognized as involuntarily unemployed persons because they own land-use rights in rural areas and can return to farm work at any time. Even in recent years, the discrimination in the labor market based on the household registration system is "not in the trend of diminishing but the trend of expanding" (Tian 2010). These forms of

---

9. *China's Urban Labor Market Research Program*, supported by the Ford Foundation, Hansheng Wang; sourced from Xie (2008).

heterogeneity of migrant labor and resident labor provide evidence for the model presented in Chapter 4, in which migrant labor and resident labor are treated as two separate production factors. Also, such heterogeneity is an important consideration in the matching function estimation discussed in Chapter 6.

On the other hand, both government and other studies done previously have recognized that rural–urban migration considerably contributes to urban economic growth (ROSC 2006; Gong et al. 2008). The most important reason for this is the substantial reduction in labor costs for enterprises through employment of rural migrants, which enlarges production scales and reinforces international competitiveness (Yan 2008; Zhao 2009). In addition, according to the search-theoretic approach, migration also encourages job creation by firms through their profit maximization. We thus incorporate these effects into our analysis.

2.3   The Dual Labor Market in Urban China

In this section, we shed light on the structure of the Chinese urban labor market. Previous studies have considered the labor market in China to be segmented into the labor markets of urban and rural areas (Knight and Song 2005). However, as the inflow of rural migrants into urban areas has increased greatly, the dual labor market within urban areas has enlarged, based on the heterogeneity of migrant and resident workers discussed in Section 2.2. This dual labor market comprises a labor market for urban residents that offers high wages, permanent jobs and government protection, and a labor market for rural migrants that provides low wages, temporary jobs, works involving less skills and limited social welfare.

The urban residents' labor market is characterized by high unemployment, as described in Section 2.1. Under the supply and demand approach discussed in Chapter 1, labor supply exceeds labor demand and thus the current wages of urban residents should be higher than the market-clearing wage, which will be estimated in detail in Chapter 3. On the contrary, rural migrants are often offered market-clearing wages because they lack government protection and union wage bargaining power. Moreover, as rural migrants possess land-use rights, jobless ones cannot be recognized as involuntarily unemployed.

This fact is consistent with the dual labor market theory demonstrated in many empirical studies, as well as similar dualisms observed outside China. Bulow and Summers (1986) explained dualism as the presence of two sectors: one sector pays wages above the market-clearing rate to discourage workers from shirking, while the other sector has no such monitoring difficulties and pays market-clearing wages. According to Piore (1980), a dual labor market can even arise within a firm that uses "a core of primary workers along with a periphery of secondary workers who were released during a slump" (Saint-Paul 1996, 3–4).

Fig. 2.7 illustrates the dual labor market in urban China. The labor market for rural migrants is measured rightward from the origin O and the labor market for urban residents is measured leftward from the origin O'. LD^{Mi}, LS^{Mi}, w^{Mi} and r^{Mi} represent the labor demand, labor supply, current wage and reservation wage of rural migrants respectively, whereas LD^{Re}, LS^{Re}, w^{Re} and r^{Re} are the labor demand, labor supply, current wage, and reservation wage of urban residents respectively. In the horizontal interval of rural migrants, the labor market is in equilibrium because their current wage w^{Mi} equals the intersection point of the labor demand curve and the labor supply curve, while in the horizontal interval of urban residents, the current wage is above the market-clearing wage w^* and thus unemployment arises.

Fig. 2.7 The dual labor market in urban China

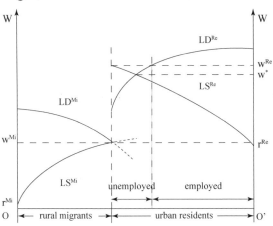

Although this model does not segment the formal and informal sectors in urban areas, we do not think that the sector segmentation, which was mentioned in some previous studies, reflects labor segmentation. In other words, there is no strong evidence to suggest that migrants are unable to work in formal settings. Indeed, 44.1% of the workers in formal construction sectors in China in 2007 were rural migrants, who also accounted for 31.2% of the workers in formal manufacturing sectors (calculated from NBS 2008a).

2.4   Job and Worker Flows

The dynamics of China's urban labor market are revealed not only by large-scale rural–urban migration but also by high job and worker flows within urban areas. The past two decades have seen dramatic job rotations and worker reallocations in urban China. Under recent economic reforms, millions of jobs in the country's SOEs have been destroyed (Wu 2005) and a large number of new jobs have been created in the private sector, especially for retrenched workers (as discussed in Sub-section 2.1.2). Such large-scale job reallocations have driven up worker mobility, leading to massive worker flows (Fig. 2.8).

Fig. 2.8 Numbers of SOEs, private enterprises and workers in these enterprise

(a) Numbers of SOEs and private enterprises (industrial enterprises)

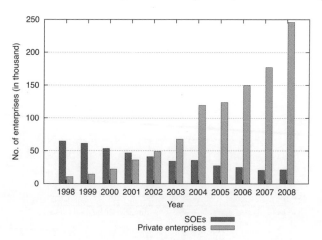

(b) Numbers of workers in SOEs and private enterprises (industrial enterprises)

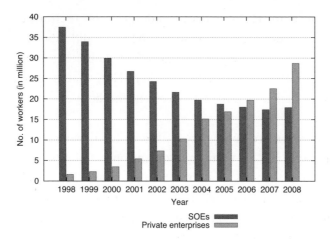

Source: NBS (1997–2009a)

Changes in the number of jobs reflect the scale of job and worker flows to some extent.[10] Fig. 2.8 shows the changes in the numbers of SOEs and private enterprises and their respective workers (note that only the industrial enterprises of *urban units*[11] are included). As shown in Fig. 2.8(a), the number of industrial enterprises in the SOE sector was 64,700 in 1998, compared with 20,700 in 2007. During the same period, the number of industrial enterprises in the private sector increased from 10,700 to 177,100. As a consequence of these job reallocations, employment in SOEs decreased by approximately 50%, while that in the private sector increased almost 20-fold. Further analysis of job and worker reallocations would need a careful measurement of job creation, destruction, and worker inflows and outflows. This will be done in Chapter 5.

---

10. These are net employment growth, and actual job and worker flows are usually larger than that (Cahuc and Zylberberg 2004).
11. For a definition of *urban units*, see footnote 2.

2.5   Job Agencies in China

Although there are many ways to undertake job recruitment, such as through social networks, company webpages, and advertisements on newspapers or TV, job agencies can often gather the most complete information on the Chinese labor market. They match jobseekers with job vacancies and thus play a key role in the delivery of labor market information.

Job agencies are easily accessible to local workers and firms in China. Each city has its own government-operated agencies as well as some private job agencies, both of which are monitored by labor bureaus. Further, unemployed residents are free to use most services provided by job agencies, and most enterprises are satisfied with the current charges for recruitment services (see Wang 2008).

China's job agencies began to develop in the early 1980s, and by 1983, they had stationed in most cities across China. In 2008, the number of job agencies was 37,208, including those run by central and local government (24,410), private job agencies (10,009), and others (2789). In 2008, 55.3 million jobseekers (including unemployed, on-the-job searchers, rural-urban migrants, and others) and 55.1 million vacant jobs were registered at job agencies, and 9.3 million unemployed workers found work through this channel, a similar number to total worker flows from registered unemployment to employment (NBS 2009a). Wang (2008) also reported that approximately 87% of enterprises used job agencies to recruit workers, including unemployed workers and rural–urban migrants.

Job agencies are the most important channel for unemployed workers to search for jobs, because such workers are outside the workplace and thus their social networks and access to information are limited. The survey by Zeng (2008) found that visiting job agencies is the most widely used and most effective approach for unemployed workers. Furthermore, job agencies are also an important channel for rural migrants, compared with obtaining job information through relatives or neighbors.

A problem for job agencies is the efficiency and quality of job-search services. Most job agencies in China still mismanage job-search information, and only a few professional staff provide a consulting service for job searches and worker recruitment. Some studies have also pointed out the blemished credit, incomplete functions and poor regulation of job agencies in China

(Wang 2008; Li 2003). Indeed, as shown in Fig. 2.9, the ratio of job agencies to urban employment had actually decreased in the past two decades, which could cause congestion and further reduce their efficiency.

Fig. 2.9 Ratio of job agencies to urban employment

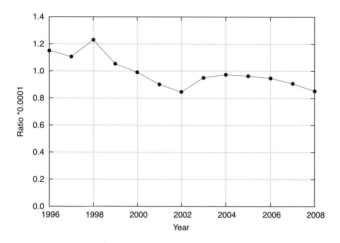

Source: NBS (1997–2009a)

In this chapter, we discussed the important characteristics of China's labor market, namely the high unemployment rate, the large number of rural migrants, the heterogeneity of migrant and resident workers, and considerable job and worker reallocations. These provide evidence for the econometric models of our study, which are constructed and estimated in Parts I and II.

Part I

The Labor Supply
and Demand Approach

3

Disequilibrium of Supply and Demand in the Labor Market of Urban Residents

3.1 Introduction

This chapter first gives an account of our application of the conventional approach to analyze China's labor market. Focuses are placed on the issues of labor supply and demand, so as to examine unemployment among China's urban residents. However, the present study does not rely solely on the variability in demand and supply, and the disequilibrium theory and corresponding models are used to analyze and describe the prevailing labor market mechanisms.

Labor demand and supply are determined by wage, non-wage income, and other factors (Cahuc and Zylberberg 2004). In a complete market, labor demand and supply stay in equilibrium based on the existence of adjustable wages. However, unemployment arises if the wage becomes rigid and is unable to respond to changes in demand and supply. The presented model thus describes a disequilibrium situation using a labor demand and supply curve, which is determined by wage, non-wage income, labor productivity and product. In the model, the wage is rigid and we find that it is significantly higher than the market-clearing equilibrium wage; this scenario results in unemployment, the extent of which is equal to the difference between supply and demand.

The rest of this chapter is organized as follows: In Section 3.2, we first review previous studies of this topic and then, in Section 3.3, we present our model of labor supply and demand. The data used are presented in Section 3.4. We use panel data analysis and a time period of 1992–2006 to examine 29 provinces in China.[1] In Section 3.5, we present the estimated

---

1. We examined provincial-level administrative regions, including Beijing, Shanghai, Tianjin, Chongqing, etc. Owing to data constraints, however, Hong Kong, Macao, Tibet, Xinjiang and Taiwan were excluded.

results and discuss the disequilibrium in unemployment in China. We then perform a brief regression in Section 3.6 so as to confirm the reaction of wages to unemployment. Finally, we make our conclusions in Section 3.7.

3.2   Literature Review

Previous studies of the causes of unemployment in China have focused on the excess of labor supply over labor demand. Although most research used descriptive analysis or merely provided statistics, a few studies did present quantitative economic analyses of the labor market in China. Most authors attributed the increasing labor supply to rapid population growth, a high rate of labor participation, and rural–urban migration (Li et al. 2001; BOJ 2008; Yang 2008). Further, views of the shortage in labor demand in China were based mainly on recognizing employment as labor demand. For instance, Li et al. (2001) and Yang (2008) defined the "employment elasticity of economic growth" as the ratio of employment growth rate to GDP growth rate. These authors found that employment elasticity decreased, especially during 1987–2000, and concluded that the need for labor in production declined during that period. Furthermore, they explained the sharp decline in labor demand by SOEs in terms of the worker retrenchment program in the 1990s.

In the same vein, Knight and Song (2005) considered worker retrenchment to be the main cause of urban unemployment. According to these authors, the economic reform has been a difficult and dangerous policy that has greatly exacerbated the unemployment problem and threatened urban workers, who had previously enjoyed preferential treatment and protection by the state. Further, Knight and Li (2006) estimated an earnings function for over 300 retrenched and reemployed workers in order to illustrate the difficulties encountered during the reemployment of retrenched workers.

In addition, we would like to draw our readers' attention that our objective is to explain unemployment at the macro level rather than the unemployment determinants for individual workers. Individual-level unemployment determinants such as education, age, gender and political capital have been well studied (Liu, Q. 2012; Knight and Song 2005; Xie 2008) and those studies have contributed to the issue of unemployment in China.

Accordingly, the fact that labor supply exceeds demand has been considered by many studies to be an important reason for the high level of unemployment in China. Beyond this apparent phenomenon, the disequilibrium theory provides reasons for unemployment on the outlook of the labor market. A theoretical model will be constructed in Section 3.3 in this regard.

3.3   Theoretical Model

Under the labor supply and demand approach, we know that $U_{it}^{Re} = LS_{it}^{Re} - LD_{it}^{Re}$, where LS_{it}^{Re} and LD_{it}^{Re} denote the social labor supply and demand of residents in province i in year t. Therefore, the main determinant is the average wage in each province. In addition, LS_{it}^{Re} is determined by non-wage income,[2] and LD_{it}^{Re} is determined by gross regional product (GRP)[3] and w_{it} / LPR_{it}, where w_{it} is current wage and LPR_{it} is labor productivity. Thus, we set

$$\ln LS_{it}^{Re} = \rho + \alpha \ln w_{it} + \beta \ln R_{it} + \varepsilon_{it}^{s}, \tag{3.1}$$

$$\ln LD_{it}^{Re} = \psi + \delta \ln \frac{w_{it}}{LPR_{it}} + \lambda Y_{it}^{T} + \varepsilon_{it}^{d}, \tag{3.2}$$

where R_{it} is non-wage income and Y_{it}^{T} is urban GRP. Moreover, ε_{it}^{s} and ε_{it}^{d} are residuals. Theoretically, the labor supply of urban residents decreases when the wage decreases and the non-wage income increases, whereas the labor demand increases when the wage decreases and the urban GRP grows,[4] which indicates that $\alpha > 0, \beta < 0, \delta < 0,$ and $\lambda > 0$.

Under the labor supply and demand approach, the number of urban unemployed residents is therefore given by

$$U_{it}^{Re} = \max[LS_{it}^{Re} - E_{it}^{Re}, 0], \tag{3.3}$$

---

2. See Cahuc and Zylberberg (2004, 9).
3. This formula is based on the theory of conditional labor demand, which minimizes cost subject to an output constraint. Thus, the regional product, Y_{it}^{T}, is also included as an explanatory variable. See Cahuc and Zylberberg (2004, 177–8) or Mas-Colell et al. (1995, 139) for more details.
4. See Cahuc and Zylberberg (2004, Chapters 1 and 4).

where U_{it}^{Re} is the number of urban unemployed residents, LS_{it}^{Re} is the resident urban labor supply, and E_{it}^{Re} is the number of urban residents who are employed.

Suppose that employment is equal to the minimum of labor demand and supply:

$$E_{it}^{Re} = \min[LS_{it}^{Re}, LD_{it}^{Re}]. \tag{3.4}$$

Since actual unemployment rates are all strictly positive, we can state that $LS_{it}^{Re} > LD_{it}^{Re}$ and $\left(LS_{it}^{Re} - E_{it}^{Re}\right) > 0.$

Thus,

$$U_{it}^{Re} = LS_{it}^{Re} - E_{it}^{Re}, \tag{3.5}$$

$$E_{it}^{Re} = LD_{it}^{Re}. \tag{3.6}$$

As a result,

$$U_{it}^{Re} = LS_{it}^{Re} - LD_{it}^{Re}. \tag{3.7}$$

Finally, the urban unemployment rate can be obtained as follows:

$$UR_{it}^{Re} = \frac{LS_{it}^{Re} - LD_{it}^{Re}}{LPO_{it}^{Re}}, \tag{3.8}$$

where $LPO_{it}^{Re} = LS_{it}^{Re}$. LPO_{it}^{Re} is the number of urban residents that participate in the labor force, which is equal to the labor supply.

From the relationship above, we finally obtain the unemployment equation as follows:

$$UR_{it}^{Re} = 1 - (\frac{w_{it}}{LPR_{it}})^{\delta} w_{it}^{-\alpha} R_{it}^{-\beta} e^{\lambda Y_{it}^T + \psi - \rho}, \tag{3.9}$$

where $\alpha > 0, \beta < 0, \delta < 0, \lambda > 0$, and $0 < (\frac{w_{it}}{LPR_{it}})^{\delta} w_{it}^{-\alpha} R_{it}^{-\beta} e^{\lambda Y_{it}^T + \psi - \rho} < 1.$

The theoretical model presented in this section indicates that in an economy where labor supply exceeds labor demand, a higher average wage leads to a higher unemployment rate, while increases in the levels of output or non-wage income decrease the unemployment rate.

3.4   Data

The annual data for labor supply, labor demand, wage and GRP are obtained from NBS (1993–2007a) and NBS (1993–2007b), which are macro data reported by the government; these data cover the 29 provinces investigated between 1992 and 2006. The National Bureau of Statistics (NBS) collects such kind of data through a statistical reporting system that collates firm-level data on product, employment and wages that are reported to local bureaus of statistics (NBS 2011a, 2011b).

For the analysis of the labor market for urban residents, the data on labor supply and demand exclude rural–urban migrants. Therefore, the method used to estimate labor supply is the same as that adopted for estimating the total labor population of urban residents in Chapter 2, namely $LS_{it}^{Re} = U_{it}^{Reg} / UR_{it}^{Reg}$, where U_{it}^{Reg} is the number of registered unemployed workers and UR_{it}^{Reg} is the registered unemployment rate. This estimation of urban labor supply includes urban residents employed in *urban units* and other workplaces such as small private enterprises, registered unemployed urban residents, and retrenched residents.

Urban labor demand is equal to the number of employed urban residents, which is calculated by excluding unemployed residents (both registered unemployed residents and retrenched residents) from the total labor population of residents; the data include urban residents who are employed in *urban units* and other workplaces. Note that we do not use the direct data on urban employment reported by NBS because they only include those people employed in *urban units*, such as SOEs, collective enterprises, foreign enterprises and other ownership enterprises, and exclude most self-employed businesses and small private enterprises.[5] Further, the data on real wages (*in yuan*) are estimated by adjusting the average nominal wages (*zaigang zhigong pingjun gongzi*) reported by NBS using a GDP deflator. The data on GRP (100 million *yuan*) are also deflated using the same GDP deflator.

We use the data on labor productivity in manufacturing industries (*yuan*) as a proxy variable of labor productivity. These data are obtained directly from the CEInet database, which is reported by the State

---

5. For instance, in 2006, the sum of the direct data on provincial employment is 111.6 million, which is much smaller than the result obtained through our method, namely 186.4 million.

Information Center.[6] Because macro data on non-wage income are difficult to gather, we use taxes on interest earned and the dividend from shares per capita (*yuan*) as proxy variables; these are available from SAT (2001–2006). Although these are not the actual values for non-wage income, provincial-level data can show regional differences in non-wage income so as to control the non-wage income effect. The descriptive statistics of the data are presented in Table 3.1.

Table 3.1 Descriptive statistics of data in resident model

	LD_{it}^{Re}	LS_{it}^{Re}	w_{it}	LPR_{it}	R_{it}	Y_{it}^T
	(persons)	(persons)	(billion *yuan*)	(billion *yuan*)	(*yuan*)	(billion *yuan*)
Mean	5,247,123	5,890,040	4962	60,454	118,473	1,865
Median	4,778,634	5,260,870	4048	53,413	76,053	1,269
Maximum	14,429,631	17,343,750	18309	158,751	554,254	13,187
Minimum	619,878	685,714	2152	17491	3,447	64
Std. Dev.	2,920,695	3,271,947	2639	31715	111,864	1,949
Observations	423	423	435	232	145	435

Sources: Data from NBS (1993–2007a); NBS (1993–2007b); SAT (2001–2006); and CEInet.

3.5   Results and Discussion

We use a fixed-effects model for the estimation. The redundant fixed-effects test (likelihood ratio) shows that the F-statistic is 268 (p = .00) and the Chi-square statistic is 607 (p = .00). Therefore, the test strongly rejects the null hypothesis that the cross-sectional effects are redundant. Thus, we prefer a fixed-effects estimation to an ordinary least squares (OLS) estimation for the subsequent analysis. Further, because the observations of our study are concerned with the 29 provinces in China, specific individual effects could influence the individual cross-sectional units. Thus, we do not make strong assumptions that such individual effects are a random group-specific disturbance, which is necessary in random-effects models (see Greene 2008, 200).

Table 3.2 shows the estimated results of urban labor supply (i.e., the fixed effects of cross-sectional units). Model 3.2.1 introduces all the

---

6.   These labor productivity data are available for only eight years, from 1998 to 2005.

possible variables, while Model 3.2.2 only includes wage. Note that in Model 3.2.1, the adjusted period is four years (2001–04) because only data on non-wage income per capita during that period are available.

Table 3.2 Estimates of the labor supply of urban residents

Independent variable	Model 3.2.1		Model 3.2.2	
	Coef.	t-stat.	Coef.	t-stat.
$\ln w_{it}$	0.23	4.54	0.06	5.20
$\ln R_{it}$	−0.09	−2.24		
Constant	14.30	26.15	14.88	151.44
Adj. R.	0.99		0.98	
F-statistic	413.8		798.6	
Period (adjusted)	2001–2004		1992–2006	
No. of observations	115		423	

The results show that wage has a statistically significant positive effect on labor supply and that non-wage income has a significantly negative effect on labor supply; these findings confirm the labor supply theory. Further, the coefficient of wage in Model 3.2.1 (0.23) is approximately three times larger than that in Model 3.2.2 (0.06), which indicates that when non-wage income is controlled, the wage effect becomes clear.

The estimates of urban labor demand are shown in Table 3.3.[7] Similar to the estimation of labor supply, Model 3.3.1 introduces all the possible variables and Model 3.3.2 only includes wage.

These results indicate that both wage (here it is wage per unit of labor productivity) and GRP are statistically significant. Consistent with the theory, labor demand declines when wage rises, and increases when GRP rises. As shown in Model 3.3.2, if the GRP factor is excluded, it is clear that there will be a misspecification.

---

7. The redundant fixed effects are strongly rejected by the test.

Table 3.3 Estimates of the labor demand for urban residents

Independent variable	Model 3.3.1		Model 3.3.2	
	Coef.	t-stat.	Coef.	t-stat.
$\ln \dfrac{w_{it}}{LPR_{it}}$	−0.16	−4.28	−0.23	−6.77
Y_{it}^{T}	3.40×10^{-5}	4.00		
Constant	14.80	203.50	14.70	188.54
Adj. R.	0.983		0.982	
F-statistic	441.2		424.0	
Period (adjusted)	1998–2005		1998–2005	
No. of observations	230		230	

Further, we examine the robustness of the estimated results generated by these two methods. First, we exclude the 10 observations that have extreme values (i.e., the five highest and five lowest values) for labor supply and labor demand, respectively, and find that the results are close to the origin estimation. Specifically, for the labor supply equation, the coefficients of $\ln w_{it}$ and $\ln R_{it}$ are 0.27*** (6.9) and −0.07* (−1.7) respectively, and for the labor demand equation, the coefficients of $\ln\,(\,w_{it}\,/\,LPR_{it}\,)$ and Y_{it}^{T} are −0.14*** (−3.8) and 3.81×10-5*** (4.13) respectively (t-statistics are in parentheses, while ***, ** and * denote statistical significance at levels of 1%, 5% and 10% respectively). Second, we examine the robustness by excluding the four observations that have extreme values for the residuals. All coefficients are again consistent with the original model, and most become even more significant. As a result, we conclude that our results are robust.

Finally, by substituting the above estimates into the model, we obtain the following unemployment equation:

$$UR_{it}^{Re} = 1 - \left(\frac{w_{it}}{LPR_{it}}\right)^{-0.16} w_{it}^{-0.23} R_{it}^{0.09} e^{3.40\times10^{-5}\,Y_{it}^{T}+0.5}, \qquad (3.10)$$

where $0 < \left(\dfrac{w_{it}}{LPR_{it}}\right)^{-0.16} w_{it}^{-0.23} R_{it}^{0.09} e^{3.40\times10^{-5}\,Y_{it}^{T}+0.5} < 1.$

Equation (3.10) indicates that unemployment is determined by wage, non-wage income and GRP. Therefore, the unemployment rate increases when wage rises and decreases when non-wage income or GRP increases.

Further, unemployment will not disappear unless the following condition is satisfied:

$$LD_{it}^{Re} \geq LS_{it}^{Re}. \tag{3.11}$$

Indeed, because non-wage income, labor productivity and GRP cannot be changed easily in the short run throughout the implementation of policy measures, we assume that they are fixed. In such cases, unemployment is determined by wage. By substituting the estimated result into the above condition, we thus obtain the following condition:

$$w_{it} \leq (LPR_{it}^{0.16} R_{it}^{0.09} e^{3.4 \times 10^{-5} Y_{it}^{T} + 0.5})^{2.56}. \tag{3.12}$$

In other words, unemployment will arise if the wage is higher than the market-clearing equilibrium wage, which can be calculated by using the equation $w_{it}^{*} = (LPR_{it}^{0.16} R_{it}^{0.09} e^{3.4 \times 10^{-5} Y_{it}^{T} + 0.5})^{2.56}$. We thus calculate it at the provincial level over the period 1998–2006 and compare it with the current wage using the equation $w_{it}^{ratio} = w_{it}^{*} / w_{it}$. The result of w_{it}^{ratio} is shown in Fig. 3.1.

In Fig. 3.1, the observations of w_{it}^{ratio} are all larger than one. Furthermore, the average of all observations of w_{it}^{ratio} is 1.57, with a standard deviation of 0.34. This indicates that the current wages of the 29 provinces during the observed period are higher than the market-clearing wages. Accordingly, for a certain rate of economic growth, labor productivity and non-wage income, the reason for the high rate of urban unemployment in China is that the current wages, which have a downward rigidity, exceed the market-clearing wages.

Fig. 3.1 Frequency of ratio of the current wage to the market-clearing wage

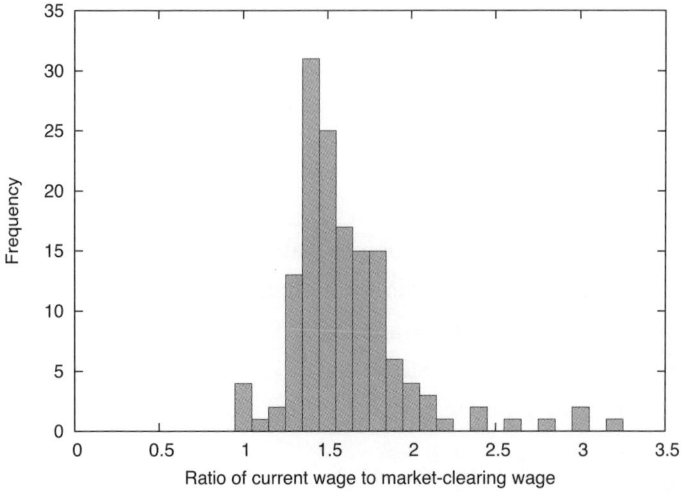

Source: Author's estimation

3.6   Response of Wages to Unemployment

In a functional labor market, growth in unemployment can cause the labor market to tighten for workers. Consequently, wages may decrease, which could reduce labor supply and increase labor demand, thus driving the disequilibrium unemployment rate downwards. Therefore, the reaction of wages to unemployment plays an important role in labor market adjustments. In this section, we thus examine the response of the wages offered to residents to urban unemployment in China. We consider the following regression equation:

$$dW_{it} = \alpha d(UR_{i,t-1}^{\mathrm{Re}}) + \beta d(Y_{it}^{T}) + \delta + \varepsilon_{it}^{uw}, \qquad (3.13)$$

where W_{it} is the real wage of province i in year t, $UR_{i,t-1}^{\mathrm{Re}}$ is the adjusted unemployment rate of province i in year $t-1$ obtained in Chapter 2, Y_{it}^{T} is the GRP of province i in year t, and ε_{it}^{uw} is a random unobservable term.

The estimated result (with the fixed effects of cross-sectional units) is as shown in Equation 3.14. The sample covers the time period 1994–2006 and includes 29 cross-sections. The total number of panel (unbalanced) observations is 364; the t-statistics are in parentheses.

$$dW_{it} = -5208.8d(UR_{i,t-1}^{\text{Re}}) + 0.9d(Y_{it}^{T}) + 321.0 + \varepsilon_{it}^{uw} \qquad (3.14)$$

$$(-6.6)*** \qquad\qquad (9.3)*** \qquad (10.6)*** \quad \text{Adj. R.}=0.49$$

The result above indicates the statistically significant negative effect of the unemployment rate on wages. If the unemployment rate increases in term $t-1$, it indicates that the excess of labor supply to labor demand increases so that firms are able to find sufficient labor at a lower wage. Consequently, in the next term t, wages decrease.

On the other hand, although wage adjustments react to unemployment changes, the scale of the reaction is slight. In the equation above, $UR_{i,t-1}^{\text{Re}}$ is a ratio and the unit of W_{it} is *yuan*; therefore, the coefficient of $UR_{i,t-1}^{\text{Re}}$ is small. Further, the adjusted R-squared value indicates that these variables explain only half of W_{it}. Accordingly, we conclude that the reaction of wages to unemployment is not sufficient to return the labor market to equilibrium.

3.7   Conclusions

The fact that labor supply exceeds labor demand in China has been observed in some previous studies. In this chapter, we looked beyond this apparent conclusion and examined the real reasons for disequilibrium unemployment based on the labor economics theory. An unemployment model that incorporated the factors of real wage, labor productivity, GRP and non-wage income was constructed in this regard. We found that the unemployment rate increases with wage rises and decreases when the non-wage income or GRP increases. Moreover, during the study period of 1992–2006, the wages for urban residents in China were higher than the market-clearing equilibrium wage, which led to unemployment. Further, we also examined the reaction of resident wages to changes in unemployment, and found that the labor market's wage adjustments to equilibrium are insufficient in China.

This chapter discussed the labor market for urban residents based on the theoretical background of labor supply and demand. However, there is another labor market in urban China, namely the labor market for rural migrants discussed in Chapter 2. We thus need to explore whether rural migrants influence the labor demand for residents. Therefore, we will use another dataset to tackle this issue of urban China in Chapter 4.

4

Does Rural-Urban Migration Reduce Labor Demand for Urban Residents?

4.1 Introduction

China has experienced large-scale rural–urban migration over recent years. By 2008, for example, the flow of migrant workers to urban areas reached 140.4 million people, approaching the total quantity of resident workers in such areas (161.7 million).[1] Based on the characteristics of migrant workers described in Chapter 2, this chapter examines how this workforce influences the urban labor market.

Previous empirical studies of the influence of rural-urban migration typically used reduced-form approaches that regressed possible factors and obtained conflicting results; structural approaches received insufficient attention in the literature. Therefore, in this chapter, we build a structural model for China's urban labor market that provides insights into the mechanism of wages, production, and labor supply and demand, as suggested by labor economics theory, so as to bridge this research gap.

The findings of the few previous studies that have addressed this issue are mainly based on reduced-form estimations. Although some of these studies have found that migrant and resident workers are direct substitutes of one another (Xie 2008; Knight and Yueh 2004, sec. 3; 2009), others have examined total employment and concluded that they are highly imperfect substitutes or complements (Knight et al. 1999; Knight and Yueh 2004, sec. 4–7; Meng and Zhang 2010).

Among these studies, Knight and Yueh (2004, sec. 3; 2009) used two attitudinal surveys: a questionnaire administered to enterprise managers in 1995 and a questionnaire administered to urban resident workers in 1999.

---

1. Among these 140.4 million rural–urban migrants, 46.7% moved to cities within their home provinces (Cai et al. 2010). The number of residents was calculated by deducting the number of migrant workers from total urban employment (302.1 million) (NBS 2009a).

The survey results showed that, in 1995, two-thirds of managers refuted the suggestion that rural workers could be replaced by unemployed urban workers, which could be used as evidence in favor of the segmentation of the labor market. In the later survey, over 50% of urban resident workers agreed that "migrants are competitors and should leave (the cities) when unemployment is high." Based on a simple regression, the researchers also concluded that competition between the two groups was increasing. Xie (2008) also based on the results of the 1999 attitudinal survey and claimed that migrants threatened the employment of urban residents.

Other studies of this topic have typically examined employment data derived from official yearbooks and enterprise surveys. For instance, Knight et al. (1999) regressed the migrant employment rate on the non-migrant employment rate and other factors, and obtained a non-significant negative coefficient, concluding that migrant and non-migrant workers were highly imperfect substitutes or even complements. Knight and Yueh (2004, sec. 4–7) also regressed the migrant employment rate on the urban unemployment rate, layoff rate and other factors, and found conflicting results among different estimation methods. Further, Meng and Zhang (2010) found a significant positive coefficient for migrants on the resident employment rate.

However, the reasons for this apparent relationship remain unclear. Knight and Yueh (2004, sec. 4–7) found that a problem with the regression used in their study was "the identification of the causal relationship." Similarly, although Meng and Zhang (2010) provided possible reasons, such as domestic economic growth and the expansion of labor demand, they did not attempt to determine causality and indicated that further study was required "to provide a conclusive explanation as to why large-scale rural–urban migration has had an non-significant impact on urban natives" Our structural model aims to address this issue.

The main theoretical background of our model uses substitutes and complements in the Hicks–Allen sense (also called p-substitutes and p-complements for brevity[2]) and gross substitutes and complements[3]

---

2. P-substitutes and p-complements are defined as the substitutes and complements of inputs for a given level of output.
3. Gross substitutes and complements take into account the determination of the optimal volume of output.

(Cahuc and Zylberberg 2004). There are three production inputs in the model presented in this chapter: migrant labor, resident labor and capital. Note that migrant labor and resident labor have been widely recognized as two separate production factors in China (Wang et al. 2005; Knight et al. 1999; Yan 2008) because of their heterogeneity (Appleton et al. 2004; Demurger et al. 2009; Knight et al. 1999), as discussed in Chapter 2. Based on this theory, migrants influence urban employment in two ways. For a given level of output, they are either p-substitutes or p-complements to residents; this is the direct influence of migrants. On the other hand, in an actual economy with endogenous output, migrant labor has a production effect, which can increase output and further expand total labor demand. Thus, the total effect, which is theoretically related to gross substitutes and complements, depends on the sum of the above two effects.

In this chapter, we examine China's urban labor market using our basic model and demonstrate a p-substitution relationship between migrant labor and resident labor at a constant level of output. This is consistent with previous findings that rural migrants compete with urban residents for jobs (Xie 2008; Knight and Yueh 2004, sec. 3; 2009). However, when considering the whole economy, our simulation results show that the production effect of migrants exceeds their p-substitution effect, which provides a reliable explanation of the apparent relationship between the two types of employments found previously (Knight et al. 1999; Knight and Yueh 2004, sec. 4–7; Meng and Zhang 2010). In short, we find that migrants create more jobs for residents than they take away from them; therefore, rural–urban migration does not contribute to urban unemployment.

The remainder of this chapter is arranged as follows: Section 4.2 outlines the theoretical framework for analysis and constructs the basic model for empirical study. Section 4.3 explains the data. Section 4.4 presents the estimation results. Section 4.5 performs the simulations and presents their results. Section 4.6 concludes.

4.2 Model

4.2.1 Mode

In an emerging economy, two types of workers exist in urban areas: urban resident workers and rural migrant workers. The labor supply and demand of urban residents (denoted by D^R and S^R respectively) and those of rural migrants (denoted by D^M and S^M respectively) comprise an inner-city dual labor market, as discussed in Chapter 2.

Of the three production inputs in the model described earlier, migrant labor and resident labor are heterogeneous factors because of the discrimination in the labor market based on the household registration system, which was introduced in Chapter 2. Given a certain production level, migrant and resident labor can therefore be substitutes or complements based on a firm's preference for cost minimization. This is termed the p-substitution effect and p-complementary effect of rural–urban migration, respectively. However, production can increase if migrants earn a lower average wage,[4] which is named the production effect of migrants herein. This production effect can expand the labor demand of residents. Thus, as mentioned above, the two effects could be negative for one and positive for the other, or positive for both. Hence, the total effect depends on the sum of these two effects.

Further, we assume resident wages to be exogenous and rigid, and migrant wages to be endogenous and flexible, for the following two main reasons. First, as shown in Chapter 3, since a labor market for urban residents that has involuntary unemployment is in disequilibrium, the wage rate, w^R, might be rigid. This wage rigidity can be explained in terms of minimum wage policies for residents or the existence of union protection. In China's case, it mainly reflects the prevailing wage system for urban residents, which is still influenced by the planned economy that ended in the 1980s and during which wages were not solely determined by the market but, to some extent, by government policies too. Although flexible

---

4. The wages of migrant workers are much lower than those of resident workers in both coastal and interior China. For instance, in 2008, the monthly wages of migrant workers in eastern, central and western China were approximately 1352, 1275 and 1273 *yuan*, respectively (Cai et al. 2010), much lower than the monthly average wages of urban workers (approximately 2611, 1954 and 2107 *yuan*, respectively) (calculated from data in NBS 2009a).

wages have then been advocated by the government, such a policy was not implemented during our sample period. Second, rural migrants are often paid market-clearing wages because they lack government protection as well as union wage-bargaining power. More importantly, as the rural migrants in China possess land-use rights and can fall back on farm work in their original rural areas, involuntary unemployment is not applicable to them.

Accordingly, in the labor market for urban residents, we assume that $U^R = S^R - D^R$, $U^R > 0$ with exogenous wages, w^R; at the same time, we assume that the labor market of rural migrants is in equilibrium, i.e. $D^M = S^M$, and that the wage is the market-clearing wage, which is endogenously determined by $D^M = S^M$.

We divide our analysis into four subsections. In the first subsection, we examine the p-substitution and p-complementary effects of migrant labor, assuming that wages, output levels and other factors remain constant. In the second subsection, we introduce determination of the output level in order to examine the production effect of migration. By combining these two effects, we obtain the total effect in the third subsection, wherein we discuss several possible cases. In the final subsection, we derive the determination equation for migrant labor and obtain the final unemployment equation.

P-Substitution and *P*-Complementary Effects of Migrants

An important outcome of migration is that migrant labor can substitute or complement resident labor at a certain output level. The theoretical background for this outcome is the conditional demand functions, which focus on how demand varies according to a rise or fall in factor prices (Cahuc and Zylberberg 2004). Given the input prices of migrant labor, w^M, resident labor, w^R, and capital, firms minimize their costs at the given output level, Q, by selecting the optimum combination of inputs. Hence, the conditional labor and capital demand functions are obtained as follows:

$$\overline{D}^R = \overline{D}^R\left(\overline{Q}, w^R, w^M, r + \delta\right), \tag{4.1}$$

$$\overline{D}^M = \overline{D}^M\left(\overline{Q}, w^R, w^M, r + \delta\right), \tag{4.2}$$

$$\overline{D}^K = \overline{D}^K(\overline{Q}, w^R, w^M, r + \delta),$$ (4.3)

where r is the real interest rate, δ is the depreciation rate, and $(r + \delta)$ is the rental price of capital. Conditional factor demand increases at lower levels of factor prices, w^R, w^M and $r + \delta$, and decreases following a reduction in the given output level, $\overline{Q}$.

As mentioned earlier, while most empirical work on the influences of migration focuses on changes in the number of workers, the conditional demand function presented enables us to look beyond this apparent phenomenon and solve the problem at a theoretical level. In Equation (4.1), for a given level of output, if $d\overline{D}^R / dw^M$ is positive or negative, rural migrants and urban residents are p-substitutes or p-complements respectively (or substitutes/complements in the Hicks–Allen sense). Accordingly, on one hand, migrants substitute or complement residents at a given level of output. However, on the other hand, they can also contribute to output and expand total labor demand, as discussed in the next subsection.

Production Effect of Migration

The notion that migration contributes to production and economic growth has been observed in many emerging economies. As Phan and Coxhead (2010) argued, economic growth and internal migration are complements: growth is a stimulus for migration and migration facilitates growth. In an empirical study in Taiwan, Burford (1970) also found that migration is an important determinant of economic development.

In China, migrants contribute to urban production based on their low wage costs (Yan 2008; Zhao 2009). Therefore, a determination equation for output level that includes analyses of migrants, residents and other factors is necessary, in order to capture how migrants affect production. Because residents exert influence on not only product supply but also product demand, based on their consumption of urban goods, we further consider both the supply and demand sides of production.

First, product supply is determined by firms' profit maximization as follows (Mas-Colell et al. 1995, 137–8):

$$\max_{L^R>0, L^M>0, K>0} \Pi = pQ(L^R, L^M, K) - (w^R L^R + w^M L^M + (r+\delta)K), \quad (4.4)$$

where $Q(L^R, L^M, K)$ is a differentiable production function and p is a given product price.

The maximization problem is solved as

$$Q^* = Q^*(w^R, w^M, (r+\delta), p). \tag{4.5}$$

We assume that p is always higher than the shut-down price. Product supply is thus given as follows:

$$S^P = S^P(w^R, w^M, (r+\delta), p) \equiv Q^*(w^M, w^R, (r+\delta), p). \tag{4.6}$$

In the next step, we examine the demand side of production. For simplicity, we assume that migrants remit all their wages to their rural homes, whereas urban residents spend all their wages on urban products. In China, migrant workers' direct spending on urban products is minimal as firms often provide them with free housing and meals, whereas urban residents stay permanently in such areas and are the main consumers of urban products.

Accordingly, product demand is obtained from the optimal consumption of urban residents. For simplicity, our analysis is presented at an aggregate level, with the total consumption of residents represented by x and average price by p. Urban residents maximize their utility, $U(x)$, subject to their income constraints, I. The optimization problem is described as follows:

$$\max_{x>0} U(x)$$

s.t. $px \leq I$. \hfill (4.7)

Solving the utility maximization problem of urban residents allows us to obtain their demand for urban products, given a certain level of income, as follows (Mas-Colell et al. 1995, 137–8):

$$x^* = x^*(p, I) \tag{4.8}$$

We assume that the income of urban residents, I, is determined by their wages, w^R, and non-wage incomes, R, as $I = I(w^R, R)$.[5] Substituting this into the solution of x^*, we obtain the determination equation of product demand as follows:

$$D^P = x^*(p, I(w^R, R)) = D^P(p, w^R, R). \tag{4.9}$$

Finally, we assume that the product market is in equilibrium, and that product price, p, is endogenous and determined by the equilibrium of product supply and demand as follows:

$$S^P(w^R, w^M, (r + \delta), p^*) = D^P(p^*, w^R, R). \tag{4.10}$$

Hence, the market-clearing price of a product is obtained as

$$p^* = p^*(w^R, w^M, (r + \delta), R). \tag{4.11}$$

Accordingly, Equations (4.6) and (4.11) lead to the final determination equation of output level, Q, given the equilibrium of the product market, as follows:

$$Q = Q^*(w^R, w^M, (r + \delta), p^*(w^R, w^M, (r + \delta), R)) \equiv Q(w^R, w^M, (r + \delta), R). \tag{4.12}$$

Note that in Equation (4.12), the effects of w^M and w^R on Q are given by the following equations respectively:

$$\frac{dQ}{dw^M} = \frac{\partial Q^*}{\partial w^M} + \frac{dQ^*}{dp^*} \times \frac{\partial p^*}{\partial w^M}, \tag{4.13}$$

$$\frac{dQ}{dw^R} = \frac{\partial Q^*}{\partial w^R} + \frac{dQ^*}{dp^*} \times \frac{\partial p^*}{\partial w^R}. \tag{4.14}$$

In these two equations, the first terms on the right-hand side are the effects of w^M and w^R on the equilibrium output level through the product

---

5. The selection of the independent variable is based on the analysis presented by Cahuc and Zylberberg (2004, 6–7). We do not identify the function as the sum of wage and non-wage incomes, because direct data on an individual's non-wage income rarely exist and a proxy variable is thus necessary.

supply side, which are negative, while the second terms on the right-hand side are their effects on output through the product demand side, which are positive. Further, we are able to show that Equation (4.13) of dQ/dw^M is negative and that Equation (4.14) of dQ/dw^R could be negative or non-negative, theoretically (see Appendix 4.C). In addition, the capital price, $(r+\delta)$, negatively affects total production (see Equations (4.4), (4.5) and (4.12)).

Above all, we obtain the production effect of migrants in China as dQ/dw^M, where

$$Q = Q(w^R, w^M, (r+\delta), R). \tag{4.15}$$

Total Effect of Migrants

The total effect of migration on the employment of residents depends on the two effects discussed above. Substituting Equation (4.15) into (4.1) thus leads to the following total labor demand function for migrants:

$$D^{R*} = D^{R*}[w^R, w^M, r+\delta, Q(w^R, w^M, (r+\delta), R)]. \tag{4.16}$$

After several calculations, we obtain the total effect of migrant wage on resident demand:

$$\left(\frac{w^M}{D^{R*}}\right)\frac{dD^{R*}}{dw^M} = \left(\frac{w^M}{D^{R*}}\right)\left(\frac{\partial D^{R*}}{\partial w^M}\right) + \left(\frac{Q}{D^{R*}}\right)\left(\frac{dD^{R*}}{dQ}\right)\left(\frac{w^M}{Q}\right)\left(\frac{\partial Q}{\partial w^M}\right). \tag{4.17}$$

In Equation (4.17), the first term on the right-hand side is the elasticity of conditional demand for urban residents with respect to migrant wages, which represents the direct effect of migrant wages on urban employment (p-substitutes or p-complements). The second term on the right-hand side represents the production effect of migrant wages on demand for residents through a change in production output.

The first term on the right-hand side of Equation (4.17) is positive or negative when the two workers are p-substitutes or p-complements respectively, while the second term is usually negative. Hence, if the estimation results of Equation (4.1) indicate that migrants and residents are complements, a decrease in migrant wages would unambiguously increase demand for residents. On the other hand, if migrants and residents were indicated as substitutes, the total effect of migration would be ambiguous. In this study, we use simulations to overcome this problem, which is theoretically based on the comparative statics of an increase in migrants relative to urban unemployment changes. The comparative statics are discussed in the last section of this chapter.

Determination of Migrant Wages and Models of the Dual Labor Market

As discussed previously, migrant wages are determined by the equilibrium in the migrant labor market, namely $D^M = S^M$. Note that since migrant labor supply is characterized by the inflows of migrants into urban areas rather than their outflows, such supply is determined by the wages for migrants, w^M, which attract rural–urban migration, and other factors, θ, that influence migration inflows, such as migration policies and job-search costs. In the model presented, θ is thus assumed to be a measure of migration acceptance. In addition, because the only income of rural migrants in urban areas is wages, non-wage income is not considered. As a result, the labor supply equation of rural migrants can be expressed as follows:

$$S^M = S^M(w^M, \theta). \tag{4.18}$$

Further, the total labor demand function of rural migrants can be obtained by Equations (4.2) and (4.15)

$$D^M = D^{M*}[Q(w^R, w^M, (r+\delta), R), w^R, w^M, r+\delta]. \tag{4.19}$$

The equilibrium condition is

$$D^M = S^M. \tag{4.20}$$

Equations (4.18) to (4.20) lead to the following equation:

$$D^{M*}[Q(w^R, w^M, (r+\delta), R), w^R, w^M, r+\delta] = S^M(w^M, \theta). \tag{4.21}$$

We define $D^M[w^R, w^M, (r+\delta), R] \equiv$
$$D^{M*}[Q(w^R, w^M, (r+\delta), R), w^R, w^M, r+\delta].$$

Therefore, the market-clearing condition is given by

$$D^M[w^R, w^M, (r+\delta), R] = S^M(w^M, \theta). \tag{4.22}$$

By solving Equation (4.22) for w^M, we obtain the determination equation for rural migrants as follows:

$$w^M = w^{M*}(\theta, w^R, (r+\delta), R). \tag{4.23}$$

For the labor market for urban residents, we assume that $U^R = S^R - D^R$, $U^R > 0$ with exogenous wages, w^R. The labor supply function of residents follows the typical form of an econometric model of labor supply:

$$S^R = S^R(w^R, R). \tag{4.24}$$

In this expression, w^R is the current wage rate, which positively influences labor supply, while R is non-wage income, which negatively affects labor supply. Further, the total labor demand function of urban residents has been obtained from Equation (4.16) as $D^{R*} = D^{R*}[w^R, w^M, r+\delta, Q*(w^R, w^M, (r+\delta), R)]$. Accordingly, under the labor demand and supply approach, the unemployment equation is given by

$$U^R = S^R(w^R, R) - D^{R*}[w^R, w^M, r+\delta, Q*(w^R, w^M, (r+\delta), R)],$$
$$U^R > 0. \tag{4.25}$$

In summary, the model of the dual labor market in urban China presented in this chapter consists of a labor market for urban residents, namely Equations (4.16), (4.24) and (4.25), and that for rural migrants, namely Equations (4.18) to (4.20), and also the determination of migrant wages, namely Equation (4.15). Further, the key equation that captures migration effect is (4.16), the empirical outcomes of which can be obtained by constructing a structural econometric model with the p-substitution or p-complementary effect of Equation (4.1), production effect of Equation (4.15), and determination of migrant wages of Equations (4.2), (4.15), (4.18) and (4.20).

4.2.2 Comparative Statics

We next examine the comparative statics of migration's contribution to urban unemployment. Since migrant labor is endogenous and can be directly increased by a migration acceptance policy, which is represented by θ in our model, we solve $dU^R / d\theta$ using Equations (4.23) and (4.25):

$$\frac{dU^R}{d\theta} = -\frac{dD^{R*}}{d\theta} = -(\frac{dD^{R*}}{dw^{M*}} \cdot \frac{\partial w^{M*}}{\partial \theta} + \frac{dD^{R*}}{dQ*} \cdot \frac{dQ*}{dw^{M*}} \cdot \frac{\partial w^{M*}}{\partial \theta}). \quad (4.26)$$

We can calculate the actual result of $dU^R / d\theta$ as long as the econometric model is straightforward. Otherwise, we can perform a simulation to obtain the result by examining the effect on D^R when increasing θ by one standard deviation. If $dD^R / d\theta$ is negative, it indicates that migration leads to higher urban unemployment, whereas if it is non-negative, migration does not contribute to, or even reduces, urban unemployment.

4.3 Data

Employing the basic dual labor market model, we used an econometric model in order to examine urban labor markets in China from 2004 to 2007, a period characterized by rapid economic growth and large-scale urban–rural migration. Three types of migration data were collected. The first one, termed Migrant Data I, provides provincial-level information on the migrant population in urban areas, as recorded by the Annual Population Changes Census of China. This survey was conducted by the Department of Population and Employment of the NBS and it covered all 31 Chinese provinces. For example, the 2007 census was carried out in 1,894 cities and 3,430 towns which were randomly selected, with 1.19 million people filling out questionnaires. Migrant Data II provides national-level information on the outflow of migrant workers, as reported by the Rural Household Survey of China (NBS 2005–2008d). The said survey is conducted every year by the Department of Rural and Social Economic Surveys of the NBS. In 2007, this department surveyed 68,000 rural households across the country. Finally, Migrant Data III provides provincial-level information on rural migrant workers in *urban units* from NBS (2005–2008a).

We therefore aimed to ascertain the data that most closely reflect the reality in the following ways:

$$E_{it}^M = T_t^M * \frac{EP_{it}^M}{\sum_{i=1}^{29} EP_{it}^M}$$

$(i = 1, \ldots, 29; t = 2004, \ldots, 2007).$ (4.27)

T_t^M is Migrant Data II in year t at the national level and EP_{it}^M is Migrant Data III, which are the numbers of rural migrant workers in urban units at the provincial level. (Using Migrant Data I instead of Migrant Data III leads to almost the same calculation results as E_{it}^M.)

We used urban GRP as the output data derived from NBS (2005–2008b). The total labor supply of urban residents, S^R, was calculated from the official urban unemployment rate and the number of unemployed people.[6] The total labor demand of urban residents, D^R, was the difference between total resident labor supply and the number of unemployed residents. These data came from NBS (2005–2008a). Since there were no direct data for capital K, we used industrial electricity as a proxy for it. The data on industrial electricity were calculated by multiplying the electricity consumption per unit of GRP, sourced from NBS (2005–2008b), by the amount of urban GRP.

Further, θ was assumed to be a measure of migration acceptance, such as the job-search assistance provided by labor exchanges for migrants. Because labor exchanges provided most job-search assistance for migrants in China, we chose the number of provincial labor exchanges as the proxy variable of θ. The data on labor exchanges were sourced from NBS (2005–2008a). Further, the proxy variable of the non-wage incomes of urban residents was taxes on interest earned and the dividend from shares, which were sourced from SAT (2005–2008).

In the next step, although no direct data existed for the aggregate wages of migrants and residents, sector-wise data on yearly wages and migrant and resident workers were reported in detail. Hence, we computed the wage rates for these two types of workers as the weighted averages

---

6. These official unemployment statistics only included urban residents.

of these sector-wise wage rates, using the shares of these workers in each sector as the weights:

$$w_{it}^R = \frac{\sum_{j=1}^{N} w_{it}^j R_{it}^j}{\sum_{j=1}^{N} R_{it}^j}, w_{it}^M = \frac{\sum_{j=1}^{N} w_{it}^j M_{it}^j}{\sum_{j=1}^{N} M_{it}^j} \tag{4.28}$$

$$(j = 1, \dots, N; i = 1, \dots, 29; t = 2004, \dots, 2007).$$

There were N sectors in province i in year t; w_{it}^R and w_{it}^M represented the wages of residents and migrants at the provincial level; R_{it}^j and M_{it}^j were the numbers of residents and migrants in sector j; and w_{it}^j was the wages paid in sector j. All data on province i in year t, such as wage, non-wage income, and GRP data, were adjusted to the standard price level of 2007. The calculation process for capital prices $(r + \delta)$ is presented in Appendix 4.A, while the data list is shown in Appendix 4.B.

4.4   Estimation

4.4.1 Methods

We estimate Equations (4.1), (4.2), (4.3), (4.15), (4.18) and (4.24) in order to describe the dual labor market in urban China. The two simultaneous estimation systems and the single estimation equation shown below are derived from those six equations:

System of factor demand functions:

$$\log D_{it}^R = \beta^{RM} \log w_{it}^M + \beta^{RR} \log w_{it}^R + \beta^{RK} \log(r_{it} + \delta_{it})$$
$$+ \beta^{RQ} \log Q_{it} + \beta^{DRdum1} dum_1 + \dots$$
$$+ \beta^{DRdum29} dum_{29} + \varepsilon_{it}^{DR}, \tag{4.29}$$

$$\log D_{it}^M = \beta^{MM} \log w_{it}^M + \beta^{RM} \log w_{it}^R + \beta^{MK} \log(r_{it} + \delta_{it})$$
$$+ \beta^{MQ} \log Q_{it} + c^{DM} + \varepsilon^{DM}, \tag{4.30}$$

$$\log D_{it}^{K} = \beta^{MK} \log w_{it}^{M} + \beta^{RK} \log w_{it}^{R} + \beta^{KK} \log(r_{it} + \delta_{it})$$

$$+ \beta^{KQ} \log Q_{it} + \beta^{DKdum1} dum_{1} + ...$$

$$+ \beta^{DKdum29} dum_{29} + \varepsilon_{it}^{DK}. \tag{4.31}$$

System of labor supply functions:

$$\log S_{it}^{M} = \beta^{SM} \log w_{it}^{M} + \beta^{\theta} \log \theta_{it} + \beta^{SMdum1} dum_{1} + ...$$

$$+ \beta^{SMdum29} dum_{29} + \varepsilon_{it}^{SM}, \tag{4.32}$$

$$\log S_{it}^{R} = \beta^{SR} \log w_{it}^{R} + \beta^{SRR} \log R_{it}^{R} + \beta^{SRdum1} dum_{1} + ...$$

$$+ \beta^{SRdum29} dum_{29} + \varepsilon_{it}^{SR}. \tag{4.33}$$

Determination equation of output level:

$$\log Q_{it} = \beta^{QM} \log w_{it}'^{M} + \beta^{QR} \log w_{it}'^{R} + \beta^{QK} \log(r_{it} + \delta_{it})'$$

$$+ \beta^{QP} \log R_{it} + c^{Q} + \varepsilon_{it}^{Q}. \tag{4.34}$$

In the estimation system, i is the cross-section of the regions and t is the time series of the years. $dum_{1}, ..., dum_{29}$ are the dummy variables of the 29 regions investigated. c in these equations are constant terms, while ε are error terms. Q is the actual output level. In Equation (4.34), $w_{it}'^{M}$ and $w_{it}'^{R}$ represent migrant and resident wages relative to worker productivity, respectively, while $\log(r_{it} + \delta_{it})'$ is the ratio of capital price to capital productivity.[7] Since China's economy grew rapidly during the sample period, it is necessary to eliminate the influences of productivity changes on output level.

Equations (4.29), (4.30), (4.31), (4.32) and (4.34) include the endogenous variables of w^{M} and Q. Thus, the most appropriate estimation method is the two-stage or three-stage least squares approaches. We next examined the relevance and exogeneity of the instrumental variables. Note that migrant acceptance θ (the number of labor exchanges) is exogenous because most labor exchanges are government-operated and manned by the

---

7. $w_{it}'^{M} = w_{it}^{M} / LP_{it}$, $w_{it}'^{R} = w_{it}^{R} / LP_{it}$, and $(r_{it} + \delta_{it})' = (r_{it} + \delta_{it}) / CP_{it}$, where LP_{it} is average labor productivity and CP_{it} is average capital productivity.

city police in China. Further, most job-search services for rural migrants are free of charge because of central or local government subsidies (GOSC 2004). Thus, there are no profitable incentives for job agencies to meet firm demand for migrant workers. For confirmation, we also ran the test for endogeneity and found that the null hypothesis of its exogeneity could not be rejected,[8] indicating that it was suitable to treat θ as exogenous.

4.4.2 Results and Discussion

Our results are reported in Table 4.1.

Table 4.1 Estimation results of the dual labor market model in urban China

	Demand (3SLS)			Supply (3SLS)		Endogenous Output (2SLS)	
	$\log D_{it}^R$	$\log D_{it}^M$	$\log D_{it}^K$	$\log S_{it}^M$	$\log S_{it}^R$		$\log Q_{it}$
Indep. Var.							
$\log w_{it}^M$	1.32	−1.38	−0.38	0.26	−	$\log w_{it}'^M$	−5.36
	(2.10)**	(−2.01)**	(−1.10)	(2.01)**	−		(−2.32)**
$\log w_{it}^R$	−1.29	1.32	0.03	−	0.23	$\log w_{it}'^R$	4.13
	(−2.00)**	(2.10)**	(1.03)	−	(3.93)***		(2.00)**
$\log(r_{it} + \delta_{it})$	0.03	−0.38	−0.02	−	−	$\log(r_{it} + \delta_{it})'$	−1.34
	(1.03)	(−1.10)	(−1.10)	−	−		(−2.90)**
$\log Q_{it}$	0.42	1.19	1.29	−	−	$\log R_{it}^R$	0.04
	(2.04)**	(11.34)***	(5.00)***	−	−		(0.07)
θ_{it}	−	−	−	0.0002	−		
	−	−	−	(1.88)*	−		
$\log R_{it}^R$	−	−	−	−	−0.01		
	−	−	−	−	(−0.17)		
Const.	11.13	5.57	5.39	10.20	11.51	*Const.*	12.40
	(9.82)***	(1.82)***	(3.25)***	(8.16)***	(42.19)***		(2.10)**
Instrumented	$\log w_{it}^M$ $\log Q_{it}$	$\log w_{it}^M$ $\log Q_{it}$	$\log w_{it}^M$ $\log Q_{it}$	$\log w_{it}^M$	−	*Instrumented*	$\log w_{it}^M$
Instruments	$\log w_{i,t-1}^M$ $\log Q_{i,t-1}$	$\log w_{i,t-1}^M$ $\log Q_{i,t-1}$	$\log w_{i,t-1}^M$ $\log Q_{i,t-1}$	$\log w_{i,t-1}^M$	−	*Instruments*	$\log w_{i,t-1}^M$
Adj. R.	0.99	0.77	0.99	0.99	0.99	*Adj. R.*	0.23

Note: T-statistics in parentheses. ***, ** and * denote statistical significance at the 1%, 5%, and 10% levels, respectively. 2SLS and 3SLS represent the two-stage and three-stage least squares estimations respectively.

---

8. The Chi-squared value of the Durbin test is 0.000 363 (p = 0.98), while the F-statistic of the Wu–Hausman test is 0.000 261 (p = 0.99).

Further, for comparison and confirmation, the results of other estimation methods are listed in Table 4.2.

Table 4.2 Comparison of different estimation methods in the dual labor market model

(a) System of Factor Demand Functions

Equation	Variable	OLS	WLS[a]	SUR[b]	2SLS	WTSLS[c]	GMM[d]	3SLS
$\log D_{it}^{R}$	$\log w_{it}^{M}$	1.53	0.41	0.40	1.54	1.34	1.44	1.32
		(4.86)***	(2.05)**	(2.00)**	(3.52)***	(2.13)**	(2.21)**	(2.10)**
	$\log w_{it}^{R}$	−1.33	−0.28	−0.26	−1.51	−1.31	−1.46	−1.29
		(−0.73)	(−0.97)	(−0.91)	(−0.87)	(−2.01)*	(−2.25)	(−2.00)**
	$\log(r_{it}+\delta_{it})$	0.02	0.03	0.03	0.03	0.03	0.03	0.03
		(0.09)	(1.07)	(1.05)	(0.14)	(1.03)	(1.26)	(1.03)
	$\log Q_{it}$	0.28	0.23	0.22	0.44	0.43	0.46	0.42
		(0.18)	(1.22)	(1.17)	(0.30)	(2.05)**	(2.38)**	(2.04)**
	Adj. R.	0.99	0.99	0.99	0.99	0.99	0.99	0.99
$\log D_{it}^{M}$	$\log w_{it}^{M}$	−1.63	−0.53	−0.52	−1.56	−1.41	−1.52	−1.38
		(−4.59)***	(−1.67)*	(−1.64)*	(−3.51)***	(−2.03)**	(−2.01)	(−2.01)**
	$\log w_{it}^{R}$	1.53	0.41	0.40	1.54	1.34	1.44	1.32
		(4.86)***	(2.05)**	(2.00)**	(3.52)***	(2.13)**	(2.21)**	(2.10)**
	$\log(r_{it}+\delta_{it})$	0.05	−0.17	−0.16	−0.09	−0.36	−0.47	−0.38
		(0.34)	(−1.75)**	(−1.67)*	(−0.23)	(−1.05)	(−1.30)	(−1.10)
	$\log Q_{it}$	1.09	1.13	1.13	1.14	1.19	1.19	1.19
		(22.38)***	(16.82)***	(16.80)***	(12.50)***	(11.30)***	(13.40)	(11.34)***
	Adj. R.	0.78	0.76	0.76	0.78	0.77	0.76	0.77
$\log D_{it}^{K}$	$\log w_{it}^{M}$	0.05	−0.17	−0.16	−0.09	−0.36	−0.47	−0.38
		(0.34)	(−1.75)**	(−1.67)*	(−0.23)	(−1.05)	(−1.30)	(−1.10)
	$\log w_{it}^{R}$	0.02	0.03	0.03	0.03	0.03	0.03	0.03
		(0.09)	(1.07)	(1.05)	(0.14)	(1.03)	(1.26)	(1.03)
	$\log(r_{it}+\delta_{it})$	−0.03	−0.03	−0.03	−0.02	−0.02	−0.01	−0.02
		(−0.14)	(−1.44)	(−1.45)	(−0.13)	(−1.12)	(−0.84)	(−1.10)
	$\log Q_{it}$	0.97	1.12	1.12	1.08	1.28	1.36	1.29
		(2.27)**	(14.17)***	(14.15)***	(2.28)***	(4.95)***	(5.02)***	(5.00)***
	Adj. R.	0.99	0.99	0.99	0.99	0.99	0.99	0.99

Note: Constants are omitted from these lists.

[a] Weighted Least Squares

[b] Seemingly Unrelated Regressions

[c] Weighted Two-Stage Least Squares

[d] Generalized Method of Moments

(b) System of Labor Supply Functions

Equation	Variable	OLS	WLS	SUR	TSLS	WTSLS	GMM	3SLS
$\log S_{it}^M$	$\log w_{it}^M$	0.11	0.11	0.10	0.26	0.26	0.26	0.26
		(1.11)	(1.29)	(1.19)	(1.61)*	(2.01)**	(2.39)**	(2.01)**
	θ_{it}	0.0002	0.0002	0.0002	0.0002	0.0002	0.0002	0.0002
		(2.70)	(3.15)***	(3.37)***	(1.51)	(1.88)*	(2.30)***	(1.88)*
	Adj. R.	0.99	0.99	0.99	0.99	0.99	0.99	0.99
$\log S_{it}^R$	$\log w_{it}^R$	0.23	0.23	0.24	0.23	0.23	0.23	0.23
		(3.36)***	(3.93)***	(4.12)***	(3.36)***	(3.93)***	(2.64)**	(3.93)***
	$\log R_{it}^R$	−0.01	−0.01	−0.02	−0.01	−0.01	−0.01	−0.01
		(−0.14)	(−0.17)	(−0.31)	(−0.14)	(−0.17)	(0.13)	(−0.17)
	Adj. R.	0.99	0.99	0.99	0.99	0.99	0.99	0.99

Note: Constants are omitted from these lists.

(c) Determination Equation of Output Level

Equation	Variable	OLS	GMM	TSLS
$\log Q_{it}$	$\log w'^M_{it}$	−1.98	−5.36	−5.36
		(−1.99)**	(−2.32)**	(−2.32)**
	$\log w'^R_{it}$	1.04	4.13	4.13
		(1.17)	(2.00)**	(2.00)**
	$\log(r_{it}+\delta_{it})'$	−0.79	−1.34	−1.34
		(−2.45)**	(−2.90)**	(−2.90)**
	$\log R_{it}^R$	0.60	0.04	0.04
		(1.51)	(0.07)	(0.07)
	Const..	6.39	12.40	12.40
		(1.61)	(2.10)**	(2.10)**
	Adj. R.	0.28	0.23	0.23

Note: T-statistics in parentheses. ***, ** and * denote statistical significance at the 1%, 5% and 10% levels respectively.

The main purpose of this chapter is to examine both the p-substitution (or p-complement) effect and the product effect of migrant labor on urban unemployment. Based on the estimation results, the econometric model is obtained as follows[9] (***, ** and * denote statistical significance at the 1%, 5% and 10% levels respectively; details of the estimations are reported in Table 4.1):

---

9. The result in Table 4.1 provides a complete description of the dual labor market in urban China. However, for the purpose of assessing the influence of migrants, only the estimates listed in the following econometric model are necessary.

$$\log D_{it}^R = 1.32 \log w_{it}^M - 1.29 \log w_{it}^R + 0.03 \log(r_{it} + \delta_{it}) + 0.42 \log Q_{it} + a_i^{dr} + \varepsilon^{DR}$$

$$\qquad (2.1) ** \qquad (-2.0) ** \qquad (1.0) \qquad\qquad (2.0) **, \qquad\qquad\qquad (4.35)$$

$$\log Q_{it} = -5.36 \log w_{it}^M + 4.13 \log w_{it}^R - 1.34 \log(r_{it} + \delta_{it})' + 0.04 \log R_{it} + 12.40 + \varepsilon_{it}^Q$$

$$\qquad (-2.3) ** \qquad (2.0) ** \qquad (-2.9) ** \qquad\qquad (0.1) \qquad (2.1)**, (4.36)$$

$$\log D_{it}^M = -1.38 \log w_{it}^M + 1.32 \log w_{it}^R - 0.38 \log(r_{it} + \delta_{it}) + 1.19 \log Q_{it} + 5.57 + \varepsilon_{it}^{DM}$$

$$\qquad (-2.0)** \qquad (2.1)** \qquad (-1.1) \qquad\qquad (11.3) *** \qquad (1.8) *,$$

$$\qquad\qquad\qquad\qquad\qquad\qquad\qquad\qquad\qquad\qquad\qquad\qquad\qquad\qquad (4.37)$$

$$\log S_{it}^M = 0.26 \log w_{it}^M + 0.0002 \log \theta_{it} + a_i^{sm} + \varepsilon_{it}^{SM}$$

$$\qquad (2.0)** \qquad\quad (1.9)*, \qquad\qquad\qquad\qquad\qquad\qquad (4.38)$$

$$D^M = S^M. \qquad\qquad\qquad\qquad\qquad\qquad\qquad\qquad\qquad\qquad (4.39)$$

In the econometric model, Equations (4.35) and (4.36) specify the two effects of migrants: the p-substitution (or p-complementary) effect and the production effect. Further, migrant wage, w^M, is endogenous and determined by Equations (4.37) (with the substitution of Equation (4.36)), (4.38) and (4.39), as $w^M = w^{M*}(\theta, w^R, (r + \delta), R)^{10}$, as discussed in Section 4.2.

The estimation results show that in Equation (4.35), the coefficients of $\log w_{it}^M$ and $\log Q_{it}$ are statistically significant and positive, which indicate that migrant labor and resident labor are p-substitutes. In other words, if migrant wages decrease, firms' demand for migrant labor would increase and that for resident labor would decrease, given other factors such as resident wages, interest rate, depreciation rate and output level. Hence, the first effect of migration on resident employment is negative. However, by contrast, in Equation (4.36), $\log w_{it}^M$ has a significant negative coefficient. This indicates that a lower level of migrant wages, which results from rural–urban migration, contributes to output level. Because the increase in output level expands the labor demand for urban residents, as shown in Equation (4.35), the product effect of rural–urban migration is positive.

---

10. Average labor productivity, LP_{it}, and average capital productivity, CP_{it}, are also included in the empirical form, because we have taken into account their influences on actual production.

In addition, all other estimates are also consistent with the theoretical model. It is shown that a higher level of resident wage, w_{it}^R, reduces labor demand for residents (Equation (4.35)), while an increase in migrant wage, w_{it}^M, leads to a lower level of migrant labor demand (Equation (4.37)). In Equation (4.36), resident wage also has a significant positive effect on output level, which indicates that its effect on product demand is larger than that on product supply, and that its effect on output is positive. Further, a higher capital price has a negative effect on output (Equation (4.36)). Finally, a higher level of migration acceptance, θ_{it}, has a significant positive effect on migration, as indicated in Equation (4.38).

In this section, we thus obtain the two effects of migration on demand for resident labor: a negative substitution effect and a positive production effect. We will then use the simulations presented in the next section to examine the total effect of migration.

4.5   Simulation

In this section, we use the econometric model presented to simulate how migration influences the labor demand for residents. The theoretical background is the comparative statics discussed previously. In our model, as the direct calculation of differentiation is complicated, we choose to use simulations.

As discussed earlier, it is inappropriate to simply increase the number of migrants because migrant labor supply is endogenous. Instead, we increase the exogenous variable θ_{it}, which is the index for the policy of migrant acceptance, by one standard deviation. This leads to a direct increase in migrant labor supply and, further, a lower level of migrant wage and a higher level of migrant demand and employment. This simulation thus lets us examine the effect on demand for residents when migration increases.[11]

The simulation result shows that for all observations, the demand for resident labor increases slightly when migration is encouraged by increasing θ_{it}. The results are summarized in Table 4.3.

---

11. We run deterministic simulations in which the equations of our econometric model are solved for each observation in the sample data, using an iterative algorithm to compute the values for the endogenous variables.

Table 4.3 Simulation results of the influence of migration

	$\log D^R$	$\log D^M$	$\log S^M$	$\log Q$	$\log w^M$
Baseline	15.385	14.732	14.732	8.581	9.700
	0.58	1.16	1.16	0.86	0.30
Scenario	15.389	14.856	14.856	8.659	9.677
	0.58	1.16	1.16	0.86	0.30
	D^R	D^M	S^M	Q	w^M
$X^{Simu} - X^{Base}$	19255	330105	330105	432	−371
$\dfrac{X^{Simu} - X^{Base}}{X^{Base}}$	0.40%	13.20%	13.20%	8.11%	−2.27%

Notes:
(1) All values are the means of observations, with their standard deviations in parentheses.
(2) X stands for each variable in the columns. For instance, $X^{Simu} - X^{Base}$ in the column of $\log D^R$ is the difference between the scenario solution and baseline solution of D^R.

Specifically, the labor demand and supply for rural migrants increased by 13.2%, and migrant wages declined by 2.3% (resident wages remained unchanged as an exogenous variable). However, firms did not reduce their total demand for resident workers; on the contrary, resident demand expanded by 0.4%. The reason is as follows: Since both resident and migrant workers are p-substitutes, when migrant wages decrease, firms substitute migrants for residents. However, the decrease in migrant wages simultaneously raises output (8.11% in our simulation result), which leads to higher demands for both types of workers. These results suggest that, concerning resident demand, the positive effect could be larger than the negative effect, because the total demand for urban residents shows an increase. Above all, the simulation results indicate that migration does not reduce labor demand for urban residents.

Note that economic growth is not the sole reason for this result. If the p-substitute effect is extremely large, or if the production effect is insufficient, migration could still reduce demand for urban resident labor and lead to urban unemployment. The influence of migration thus depends on the comparative sizes of the p-substitution and production effects in the actual situation.

In summary, as the estimation and simulation results indicate, although migrants and residents in China are p-substitutes at a given level of output, the expansion of migration does not reduce the demand for residents across the whole economy. Rather, the low cost of migrant work could contribute to economic growth and enlarge the total demand for labor.

4.6   Conclusions

This chapter provided a structural approach for examining the influences of rural–urban migration on urban areas in developing countries. The construction of an inner-city dual labor market model led to two main findings. First, the influence of migration on the employment prospects of urban residents is a combination of both the p-substitution or p-complementary effect and the production effect. The total effect can thus be derived from the resident labor demand function, the determination equation of output level, and the equilibrium of migrant labor demand and supply functions. Second, depending on the actual situation, rural–urban migration could either increase or decrease the unemployment rate of urban residents.

Using the model presented, we then estimated an econometric model of China's dual labor market in urban areas and ran simulations to examine the total effect of migrant labor on resident demand. The resident labor demand estimation indicates that a decrease in migrant wages leads to a lower level of resident demand if other factors remain unchanged, implying that resident and migrant workers are p-substitutes. However, when considering endogenous output level and the whole dual labor market with our model, we found that migrant employment increases labor demand for urban residents because the lower cost of migrant workers contributes to economic growth and thus higher total labor demand.

Although our study is the first to apply structural models in order to address this issue, some local governments have already recognized the contribution of migration and eased restrictions in recent years. In 2007, for example, many large Chinese cities stopped charging migration fees. Further, in 2009, Guangdong and Hunan, among other provinces, held free recruitment meetings for rural migrants to encourage them to work in cities. Importantly, excessively strict migration restrictions do not provide residents effective protection from unemployment, and could even cost the city the chance to improve employment and economic development.

In this chapter, we examined the influences of rural–urban migration on the urban labor market using the labor supply and demand theory. The conclusion that migration does not contribute to urban unemployment drawn in this chapter can also be concluded from our work based on search and matching theory, which will be included in our analysis of labor-market matching and job creation in Chapters 6 and 7 respectively.

Part I of this book concentrates on labor supply and demand in China's urban labor market, the imbalance of which has long been regarded as an important reason for the high level of national unemployment. However, as in most developed countries, the labor market in China also has imperfect information because of the frictions arisen from high degrees of job and worker reallocation. Therefore, the process that moves from job search and vacancies to employment plays an important role in the labor market. Accordingly, Part II will examine these aspects from the perspective of search and matching theory.

Appendix 4A Calculation and Confirmation of Capital Price Data

The data on capital prices, $(r + \delta)$, are calculated according to the following steps. First, we calculate the GRP deflators (%) and inflation rates. The data on nominal GRP (GRP_{it}^{*}) and the real GRP index (GRP_{it}^{index}) are available from NBS (2005–2008a). The real GRP index in China is defined as

$$GRP_{it}^{index} = \frac{GRP_{it}^{re}}{GRP_{i,t-1}^{re}},\tag{4.40}$$

where GRP_{it}^{re} is the real GRP of region i in year t.

The GRP deflator is defined as

$$GRP_{it}^{deflator} = \frac{GRP_{it}^{*}}{GRP_{it}^{re}} * 100,\tag{4.41}$$

where we assume that the price in year $t - 1$ is 1 and $GRP_{i,t-1}^{*} = GRP_{i,t-1}^{re}$.

Using GRP_{it}^{*} and GRP_{it}^{index}, the GRP deflator (%) is calculated as

$$GRP_{it}^{deflator} = \frac{\dfrac{GRP_{it}^{*}}{GRP_{i,t-1}^{*}}}{GRP_{it}^{index}} * 100. \tag{4.42}$$

As a result, we have the following inflation rates, g_{it}^{p}:

$$g_{it}^{p} = (\frac{GRP_{it}^{deflator}}{100} - 1) * 100\%. \tag{4.43}$$

The second step is to find out the depreciation rate, δ_{it}. Although only data on the depreciation amount D_{it}^{*} and fixed investment I_{it}^{*} of current prices are available, they enable us to ascertain an approximate value of the depreciation rate:

$$KF_{it} = KF_{i,t-1} - D_{i,t-1} + I_{it}, \tag{4.44}$$

$$KF_{i,t-1} = KF_{i,t-2} - D_{i,t-2} + I_{i,t-1}, \tag{4.45}$$

$$KF_{i1} = KF_{i0} - D_{i0} + I_{i1}, \tag{4.46}$$

where KF_{it} is the capital stock of province i in year t, $D_{i,t}$ is the amount of depreciation in province i in year t, and I_{it} is the capital investment of province i in year t.

This leads to

$$KF_{it} = KF_{i0} - (D_{i0} + ... + D_{i,t-1}) + (I_{i1} + ... + I_{it}). \tag{4.47}$$

The data cover 1993 to 2007, and the capital stock of $KF_{i,2007}$, $KF_{i,2006}$, $KF_{i,2005}$ and $KF_{i,2004}$ is directly needed for this study:

$$KF_{it} = KF_{i,1993} - (D_{i,1993} + ... + D_{i,t-1}) + (I_{i,1994} + ... + I_{it}), \tag{4.48}$$

where t = 2004, 2005, 2006 and 2007.

Further, $KF_{i,1993}$ can be ignored because its value is small compared with $-(D_{i,1993} + ... + D_{i,t-1}) + (I_{i,1994} + ... + I_{it})$.

As a result,

$$KF_{it} \approx -(D_{i,1993} + ... + D_{i,t-1}) + (I_{i,1994} + ... + I_{it}. \tag{4.49}$$

We calculate the right-hand side as follows. Assuming that the price in 2007 is 1, we have

$$D_{i,07} = D^*_{i,07}, \tag{4.50}$$

$$D_{i,06} = D^*_{i,06}(1 + g^p_{i,07}), \tag{4.51}$$

$$D_{i,05} = D^*_{i,05} * (1 + g^p_{i,07}) * (1 + g^p_{i,06}), \tag{4.52}$$

$$D_{i,04} = D^*_{i,04} * (1 + g^p_{i,07}) * (1 + g^p_{i,06}) * (1 + g^p_{i,05}). \tag{4.53}$$

$$\vdots$$

This is the same as I_{it}. Finally, the depreciation rate is obtained as

$$\delta_{it} = \frac{D_{it}}{KF_{it}}, \tag{4.54}$$

where t = 2004, 2005, 2006 and 2007.

In the last step, the real interest rate, r_{it}, is easily obtained by

$$r_{it} = r^*_{it} - g^p_{it}, \tag{4.55}$$

where r^*_{it} is the nominal interest rate and g^p_{it} represents the inflation rates calculated above.

The data on r^*_{it} are the averages of all nominal interest rates in year t, including the three-month rate, six-month rate, one-year rate, and so on.

To test the reliability of our estimated data, we calculate the input of the capital-to-labor ratio, K_{it} / L_{it}. Capital input, K_{it}, is calculated as $K_{it} = KF_{it} * (r_{it} + \delta_{it})$, while labor input, L_{it}, is obtained from $L_{it} = w^R_{it} * E^R_{it} + w^M_{it} * E^M_{it}$, where w^R_{it} and w^M_{it} are the calculated wages of residents and migrants respectively. K_{it} / L_{it}, which is derived from the estimated data, is described in Fig. 4.1. In the official GDP and GRP statistics, there are direct capital input and labor input data. The capital-to-labor ratio $K_{it}^{GRP} / L_{it}^{GRP}$ is shown in Fig. 4.2.

Fig. 4.1 K_{it} / L_{it} according to the calculated data

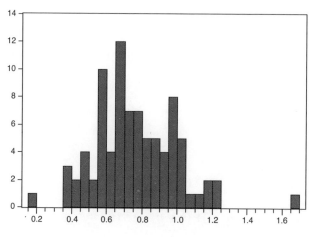

Source: Author's calculation.

Fig. 4.2 $K_{it}^{GRP} / L_{it}^{GRP}$ according to the GRP data

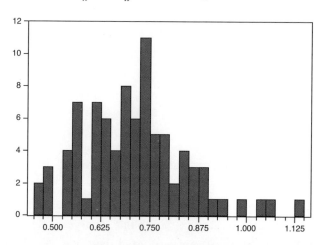

Source: Author's calculation.

Figs. 4.1 and 4.2 show no noticeable disparities between our calculated data and the official GDP data. Moreover, we obtain 0.76 as the mean of all observations of K_{it} / L_{it}. This is close to that of $K_{it}^{GRP} / L_{it}^{GRP}$, which is 0.71.

Further, since we use data on regional industrial electricity as the proxy variable for capital input D_{it}^K, we also test the calculated capital stock data by regressing with the regional industrial electricity data, namely $KF_{it} = \alpha D_{it}^K + \chi$. The adjusted R-squared value of the panel least squares is 0.84 and the t-statistic of the coefficient α is 21.6. These results indicate a strictly close relationship between the proxy variables and calculated capital stock. Accordingly, the calculated data are reliable for the estimation.

Appendix 4B Main Data List

The main data list is given in Table 4.4.

Table 4.4 Descriptive statistics of data in the dual labor market model

	D^R	S^R	E^M	D^K	w^R	w^M	$(r+\delta)$	Q
	(persons)	(persons)	(persons)	(10^6 kw/h)	(yuan)	(yuan)	(%)	(billion yuan)
Mean	5813887	6459616	4478602	86532.35	22380.76	16836.89	10.32	731.26
Med	5527525	6219784	2619352	59320.32	20246.93	15587.61	10.23	532.19
Max	13763024	14480000	20322882	321408.60	51472.66	39456.13	16.67	2938.89
Min	862397	923664	97494	5418.78	12981.99	10609.20	1.95	54.28
S.D.	3320567	3640403	4853612	67900.48	7509.34	5030.34	2.72	630.25
Obs.	86	86	86	86	86	86	86	86

Appendix 4C Theoretical Signs of dQ/dw^M and dQ/dw^R

In the theoretical model, we found that Equation (4.13) of dQ/dw^M is negative and that Equation (4.14) of dQ/dw^R could be negative or non-negative, according to the following steps. First, Equation (4.6), $S^P = S^P(w^R, w^M, (r+\delta), p) \equiv Q*(w^M, w^R, (r+\delta), p)$, and Equation (4.10), $S^P(w^R, w^M, (r+\delta), p*) = D^P(p*, w^R, R)$, lead to the following equation:

$$Q*(w^M, w^R, (r+\delta), p*) = D^P(p*, w^R, R). \qquad (4.56)$$

We denote an implicit function, $A(w^M, w^R, (r + \delta), p*, R)$, which is defined as

$$A(w^M, w^R, (r + \delta), p*, R) = Q*(w^M, w^R, (r + \delta), p*)$$
$$- D^P(p*, w^R, R)$$
$$= 0. \qquad (4.57)$$

Thus, the next two conditions are satisfied based on Equation (4.57). Note that here $p*$ is considered to be an exogenous variable in the implicit function of $A(w^M, w^R, (r + \delta), p*, R)$:

$$\frac{dp*}{dw^M} = -\frac{\dfrac{dA}{dw^M}}{\dfrac{dA}{dp*}} = -\frac{\dfrac{\partial Q*}{\partial w^M}}{\left(\dfrac{\partial Q*}{\partial p*} - \dfrac{\partial D^P}{\partial p*}\right)}, \qquad (4.58)$$

$$\frac{dp*}{dw^R} = -\frac{\dfrac{dA}{dw^R}}{\dfrac{dA}{dp*}} = -\frac{\left(\dfrac{\partial Q*}{\partial w^R} - \dfrac{\partial Q*}{\partial w^R}\right)}{\left(\dfrac{\partial Q*}{\partial p*} - \dfrac{\partial D^P}{\partial p*}\right)}. \qquad (4.59)$$

Then, we rewrite Equations (4.58) and (4.59) as follows:

$$\frac{\partial Q*}{\partial w^M} + \frac{\partial Q*}{\partial p*} \times \frac{dp*}{dw^M} = \frac{\partial D^P}{\partial p*} \times \frac{dp*}{dw^M}, \qquad (4.60)$$

$$\frac{\partial Q*}{\partial w^R} + \frac{dQ*}{dp*} \times \frac{\partial p*}{\partial w^R} = \frac{\partial Q*}{\partial w^R} + \frac{\partial D^P}{\partial p*} \times \frac{dp*}{dw^R}. \qquad (4.61)$$

Because $\partial D^P / \partial p* < 0$, $dp* / dw^M > 0$, and $\partial Q* / \partial w^R > 0$, we find that the sign of the right-hand side of Equation (4.60) is negative, while that of the right-hand side of Equation (4.61) could be negative or non-negative, depending on the actual situation.

Finally, from the formulation of Equation (4.12), with the definition of endogenous $p*$ from Equations (4.10) and (4.11), the left-hand sides of Equations (4.60) and (4.61) are equivalent to the right-hand sides of Equations (4.13) and (4.14) respectively. As a result, Equation (4.13) of dQ / dw^M is unambiguously negative, while Equation (4.14) of dQ / dw^R could be negative or non-negative.

Appendix 4D A Confirmation with a Reduced-form Estimation

To confirm the structural estimation result, we ran a reduced-form estimation, with the following result:

Table 4.5 Confirmation with a reduced-form estimation

Dependent variable: $\log D_{it}^R$

	OLS	2SLS	GMM
Indep. Var.			
$\log w_{it}^R$	0.15	0.21	0.21
	(0.51)	(0.71)	(0.71)
$\log(r_{it} + \delta_{it})$	0.62	0.59	0.59
	(3.96)***	(3.70)***	(3.70)***
$\log R_{it}$	0.18	0.12	0.12
	(0.63)	(0.42)	(0.67)
$\log \theta_{it}$	0.51	0.59	0.59
	(9.48)***	(10.05)***	(10.05)***
Const..	7.60	6.97	6.97
	(4.13)***	(3.72)***	(3.72)***
Instrumented	–	$\log \theta_{it}$	$\log \theta_{it}$
Instruments	–	$\log \theta_{i,t-1}$	$\log \theta_{i,t-1}$
Adj. R.	0.59	0.58	0.58

Note: T-statistics in parentheses. ***, ** and * denote statistical significance at the 1%, 5% and 10% levels, respectively. 2SLS = two-stage least squares estimation. GMM = generalized method of moments.

The result indicates that migrant acceptance, θ, has a significant positive effect on labor demand for residents, $\log D_{it}^R$, which is consistent with our final simulation result.

Part II

The Search-Theoretic Approach

5

Facts about Job and Worker Reallocations

5.1 Introduction

China's urban labor market over the past two decades has been characterized by dramatic reallocations of jobs and workers. The enterprise reforms of the 1990s destroyed millions of jobs in SOEs and created a large number of new positions in the private sector. This led to large-scale job rotations and worker reallocations, with workers flowing from SOEs to private enterprises, from employment to unemployment, and from one industrial sector to another, as well as a large number of migrant workers flowing from rural farms to urban firms. This chapter describes these job and worker reallocations in China in detail.

One measurement of job creation and destruction is firm-level employment changes (Davis and Haltiwanger 1996; Deng et al. 2005). In the literature, job creation is generally considered to take place when a firm is formed or expanded, whereas job destruction occurs when a firm is closed or it contracts out jobs. However, some studies consider that job reallocation also includes those reallocations within the same firm. In such cases, the overall workforce of the firm remains unchanged. For instance, a technical worker's job could be replaced by a managerial job (Cahuc and Zylberberg 2004; Hamermesh et al. 1996; Lagarde et al. 1995). In our study, we employ worker-related data in order to examine both sides of the job reallocation process. In other words, when a firm hires a new worker, it means the creation of a job, whereas when a firm terminates a worker's contract for any reason, it means the destruction of a job.

Worker flows are usually larger than job flows because of job-to-job worker transfers and new hires recruited into positions that are held by workers about to retire (Cahuc and Zylberberg 2004). Worker flows out of certain employment lead to unemployment, non-participation in the workforce, or job-to-job transfers to other workplaces; worker flows into certain employment comprise flows from outside the local labor market (e.g., rural–urban migration or recruitment of fresh graduates) as well as from inside the local labor market (e.g., job-to-job worker transfers and hiring of unemployed workers).

Our dataset covers all industries in urban China, including manufacturing, construction, IT, education services, health services, and financial services. These industries are divided into three ownership-based sectors: the state-owned sector (SOEs), the collective sector, and the private sector. In our study, the private sector is a widely defined category, including all enterprises that are not owned or controlled by the state or the collective sector, such as joint-ownership enterprises, limited liability corporations, foreign enterprises, and small individual enterprises (including self-employed persons; *siyingqiye* and *getihu* in Chinese).

Although a considerable amount of statistics on employment in China exists, so far no previous study has classified and adjusted these data based on the labor economics theory. The presented data on job and worker flows were derived mainly from the following datasets: "Increase in Employment" and "Decrease in Employment" in *state-owned units*, *collective-owned units* and *other ownership units*. These datasets provide data on recruitments, firings, contract endings, etc. in *urban units*. Some adjustments to the data were necessary owing to missing information. These data were sourced from NBS (1992–2010a) and the CEInet database.

The remainder of this chapter is designed as follows: Section 5.2 describes job reallocations, Section 5.3 discusses worker inflows and outflows, and Section 5.4 concludes.

5.2   Job Reallocations

In this section, we examine annual job reallocations for the period 1991–2009 at both the national level and the level of the ownership-based sector. As discussed in Section 5.1, job reallocations were influenced by two noteworthy changes during the period investigated: (i) the decline of the state-owned sector during the late 1990s, and (ii) the continuous expansion of the private sector. Further, it is important to note that job reallocations can occur within a single sector or between sectors (Cahuc and Zylberberg 2004).

5.2.1 Job Creation and Destruction at the National Level

The job creation in period t is defined as the sum of all new positions created by firms and filled by workers[1] between the ends of periods t and $t - 1$:

$$JC_{it} = TR_{it} - RE_{it} + EI_{it} + OC_{it},$$ (5.1)

where TR_{it} stands for total recruitment, RE_{it} represents the recruitment that replaces retirees, EI_{it} is the excess of transfer inflows over transfer outflows of all firms, and OC_{it} represents other job creations, such as those through self-employment.

Furthermore, the job destruction in period t is defined as the sum of all existing positions lost in all firms between the end of periods t and $t - 1$:

$$JD_{it} = FI_{it} + CE_{it} + LA_{it} + EO_{it} + OD_{it},$$ (5.2)

where FI_{it} represents firings, CE_{it} represents contract endings, LA_{it} represents layoffs, EO_{it} is the excess of transfer outflows over transfer inflows, and OD_{it} represents other job destructions, such as that caused by the death of an employed worker.

Further, we also evaluate *net employment growth*, *job reallocations* and *excess job reallocations* as follows. According to previous studies (see Cahuc and Zylberberg 2004; Davis and Haltiwanger 1996), the *net employment growth* in period t is the difference between the employment levels at the end of periods t and $t - 1$. The net employment growth rate thus equals the job creation rate minus the job destruction rate. *Job reallocation* is measured as the sum of job creation and job destruction, while *excess job reallocation* is measured as the difference between job reallocation and the absolute net employment change in period t. (See Table 5.1.)

Fig. 5.1 shows that, as in most countries, the rates of job creation and job destruction are much larger than the absolute net employment growth rate. For instance, in 1998, the absolute net employment growth rate was 2.8%, while the job destruction and job creation rates were 9.4% and 6.5% respectively, resulting in an annual job reallocation rate of 15.9%.

---

1. In this chapter, job creation excludes jobs that are not filled by workers within a year.

The job creation rate fluctuated around 5% during the 1990s, but began to rise rapidly around the turn of the century and surpassed 10% by the late 2000s. This rising trend in the second half of the period of study occurred because of the comparatively high level of productivity, which increased expected profits for firms (also called the capitalization effect) and lowered the rate of job destruction. This trend led to a longer lifetime for jobs, so that firms could expect more returns when creating jobs. By contrast, job destruction started to increase quickly from 1991, peaked in 1998, and decreased gradually thereafter because of the impact of the enterprise reform at that time (see Section 5.2.2).

Job reallocations generally showed trends that were similar to those of job destruction and creation before 2000, but kept on growing thereafter despite a decrease in job destruction. The continued growth after 2000 was caused by very rapidly growing job creations.

Fig. 5.1 Job creation and destruction rates in urban China

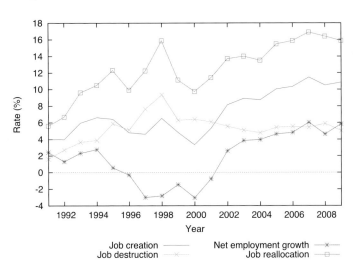

Source: Author's calculation from NBS (1992–2010a)

Notes: These statistics are concerned with employment in *urban units*; hence, self-employment and employment in small and informal firms are excluded. The rates of job creation and destruction are annual rates as percentages of total employment.

Table 5.1 Job reallocation in urban China

	JC	JD	NEG	JR	EJR	Proportion of Job Reallocation between Sectors	
						Industrial Sector	Ownership Sector
1991	4.02%	1.60%	2.42%	5.61%	3.20%	0.00	0.00
1992	4.00%	2.69%	1.30%	6.69%	5.39%	0.02	0.00
1993	5.97%	3.65%	2.32%	9.62%	7.30%	0.38	0.00
1994	6.62%	3.87%	2.75%	10.50%	7.75%	0.18	0.12
1995	6.44%	5.87%	0.57%	12.31%	11.74%	0.04	0.44
1996	4.81%	5.12%	−0.31%	9.93%	9.62%	0.22	0.37
1997	4.63%	7.63%	−3.00%	12.26%	9.26%	0.14	0.66
1998	6.54%	9.35%	−2.81%	15.88%	13.07%	0.30	0.69
1999	4.84%	6.30%	−1.46%	11.14%	9.67%	0.06	0.47
2000	3.36%	6.40%	−3.04%	9.75%	6.71%	0.05	0.51
2001	5.32%	6.09%	−0.77%	11.42%	10.65%	0.07	0.43
2002	8.16%	5.56%	2.60%	13.72%	11.12%	0.10	0.36
2003	8.93%	5.08%	3.85%	14.02%	10.17%	—	0.23
2004	8.75%	4.78%	3.97%	13.53%	9.55%	0.05	0.14
2005	10.06%	5.42%	4.64%	15.49%	10.85%	0.05	0.11
2006	10.35%	5.53%	4.82%	15.88%	11.06%	0.02	0.05
2007	11.47%	5.43%	6.04%	16.90%	10.86%	0.01	0.00
2008	10.52%	5.89%	4.63%	16.41%	11.78%	0.02	0.00
2009	10.87%	5.02%	5.84%	15.89%	10.04%	0.00	0.00

Note: NEG= Net Employment Growth; JR= Job Reallocation; EJR= Excess Job Reallocation.

Source: Author's calculation from NBS (1992–2010a)

5.2.2 Job Creation and Destruction by Ownership Group

The rates of job creation and destruction differed among the three earlier identified ownership-based groups (see Fig. 5.2) because the worker retrenchment program was limited to the state-owned and collective sectors. This program considerably reduced the surplus employment created by the planned economy in both of these sectors.

Fig. 5.2 Employment scales of state-owned, collective and private sectors

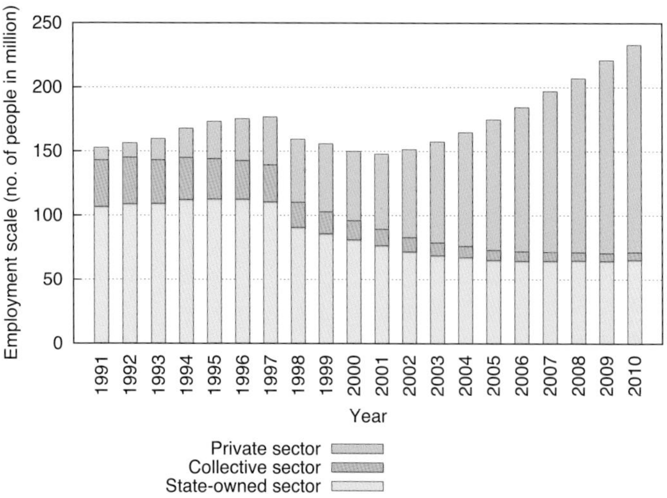

Source: NBS (1992–2011a)

Figs. 5.3 and 5.4 show the rates of job creation, job destruction, job reallocation and net employment growth by ownership group. As shown in Fig. 5.3, the job destruction rates in the state-owned and collective sectors increased in the 1990s, peaked in 1998, and dropped back in the 2000s. By contrast, job destruction in the private sector gradually increased throughout the period of study (Fig. 5.4).

However, the job creation trends are similar in all three sectors: they decreased during the 1990s and then tended to increase during the 2000s. Job creation was particularly active in the private sector in the 2000s. For instance, in 2005, the job creation rate in the private sector was 7.3% even if we ignored small individual firms, but would rise to at least 14.4% if such firms were included. This high rate of 14.4% is still a lower bound of job creation because the statistical system for small individual firms is incomplete in China, and also because our calculation of job creation in small firms represents only net employment growth (this is also the reason for the unregulated changes in Fig. 5.4(b)).

Fig. 5.3 Job reallocations in the state-owned and collective sectors
(a) State-owned sector

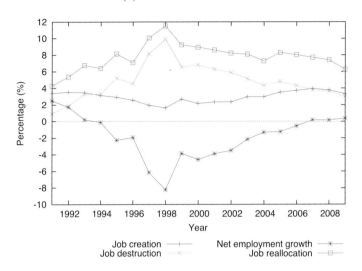

(b) Collective sector

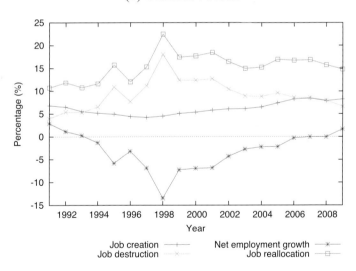

Source: Author's calculation from NBS (1992–2010a).

Note: The rates shown are percentages of employment in each ownership sector.

Fig. 5.4 Job reallocation in the private sector
(a) Private sector without small-scale individual firms

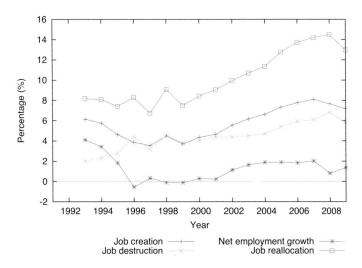

(b) Private sector with small-scale individual firms

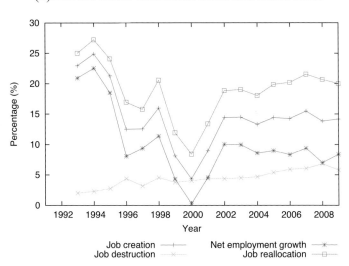

Source: Author's calculation from NBS (1992–2010a).

Note: The rates shown are percentages of employment in each ownership sector.

5.2.3 Intra-sector and Inter-sector Reallocations by Ownership and Industrial Sectors

As discussed in Section 5.1, job reallocations between ownership sectors mainly occurred because of the enterprise reforms in China that destroyed inefficient jobs in SOEs and the subsequent industrial restructuring process. However, as some job reallocations could simply arise from net employment changes, we introduce a definition of excess job reallocation in order to separate this proportion of reallocations from those taking place within or between sectors. Excess job reallocation, denoted by T^E, thus represents the proportion of job reallocations over the amount required to accommodate net employment changes that can occur within or between sectors (Davis and Haltiwanger 1996), and it is calculated as $T^E = T - |V_n|$, where T denotes total job reallocation and V_n denotes net employment growth in the entire economy.

Following the approaches of Cahuc and Zylberberg (2004) and Davis and Haltiwanger (1992), we denote net employment growth in a given sector s by V_n^s, and denote net employment growth in the entire economy by V_n. Therefore, the extent of inter-sector job reallocations, denoted by R_E, is defined by the following equation:

$$R_E = \sum_{s=1}^{S} |V_n^s| - |V_n|. \tag{5.3}$$

Job reallocations in sector s are denoted by T_s. The sum of excess job reallocations within each sector, denoted by R_I, is given by

$$R_I = \sum_{s=1}^{S} (T_s - |V_n^s|). \tag{5.4}$$

Note that the term $\sum_{s=1}^{S} T_s$ in the above equation is actually the total job reallocation in the economy, which is denoted by T. Hence, Equation (5.4) can be rewritten as

$$R_I = T - \sum_{s=1}^{S} |V_n^s|. \tag{5.5}$$

Finally, the proportion of inter-sector reallocations is measured by the ratio $R_E/(R_I + R_E)$. We calculate the annual ratios of inter-sector reallocations for the industry-based and ownership-based sectors separately (see Table 5.2). As in most other countries, the average annual ratio of inter-sector reallocations is a minor proportion of total excess job reallocations in China, namely 0.10 for industry-based sectors and 0.21 for ownership-based sectors. The inter-sector reallocation for ownership-based sectors is a little higher in China following the country's enterprise reforms. However, the upper levels of all annual rates are extremely high, namely 0.38 for industry-based sectors and 0.56 for ownership-based sectors. This finding implies a period when inter-sector reallocations were particularly active. Based on the foregoing, Fig. 5.5 illustrates the annual ratios of inter-sector reallocations to total excess reallocations, denoted by $R_E/(R_I + R_E)$, for each year (these values are reported in Table 5.2).

Table 5.2 Proportion of inter-sector reallocations

Country	Period	Number of sectors	$R_E/(R_I + R_E)$		
China	1991–2009	15	Aver.	Max.	Min.
	(annual rate)	(industry based)	0.10	0.38	0.00
China	1991–2009	3	Aver.	Max.	Min.
	(annual rate)	(ownership based)	0.21	0.56	0.00
Germany	1989–1990	24	0.03		
United States	1972–1988	980	0.14		
France	1984–1988	15	0.06		
France	1984–1991	28	0.17		
Italy	1986–1991	28	0.02		

Source: The values for China were calculated by the author. The values for other countries were taken from Cahuc and Zylberberg (2004) and Davis and Haltiwanger (1999, Table 5).

Fig. 5.5 shows that the proportion of reallocations between ownership sectors (relative to total excess reallocations) was high in the period 1994–2002 because of the enterprise reforms. Further, it is shown that job reallocations between the 15 main industrial sectors were high in the 1990s, reflecting the fact that industry restructuring was especially notable in this period. After 2002, although the total job reallocation rate continued to grow, the proportion of reallocations between sectors dropped significantly, indicating that the excess job reallocations in the 2000s were mainly caused by intra-sector reallocations.

Fig. 5.5 Annual inter-sector reallocation ratio to total excess reallocation

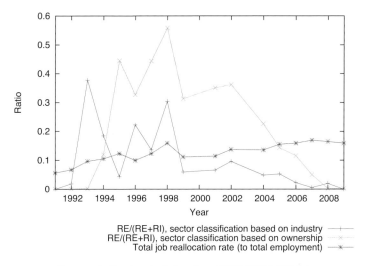

Source: Author's calculation from NBS (1992–2010a)

5.2.4 Relations between Job Creation/Destruction and the GDP Growth Rate

In developed countries, the relations between job creation/destruction and business cycles often draw much attention. For instance, in OECD countries, job destruction is generally counter-cyclical and job creation pro-cyclical (see OECD 1996; Cahuc and Zylberberg 2004). However, in the US, although job destruction is highly counter-cyclical, job destruction is weakly pro-cyclical or even non-cyclical (Davis and Haltiwanger 1996). In this section, we thus examine the relations between job creation/destruction and annual changes in the real GDP growth rate.

Fig. 5.6 confirms that changes in job creation generally coincide with changes in the GDP growth rate, and that changes in job destruction are generally opposite to changes in the GDP growth rate; these are similar to the relationships between job creation, job destruction and business cycles in developed countries.

Some studies have claimed that China's rapid economic growth has not contributed to employment growth (see Yang 2008). Indeed, Fig. 5.1 showed that employment grew only slightly during the period of study even though the real GDP maintained a growth rate of over 7.6% (employment even experienced negative growth during 1997–2000). However, changes in gross employment do not represent the real contribution of economic growth to employment, because economic growth directly affects job creation in particular. As shown in Fig. 5.6, job creation maintained a positive growth rate during this period, consistent with the accompanying positive economic growth. (The notable exception in 1998 could have been caused by the sharp increase in the quantity of unemployed workers, which loosened the tightness of the labor market and encouraged firms, especially those in the private sector, to create more jobs.)

Fig. 5.6 Job creation, job destruction and GDP growth

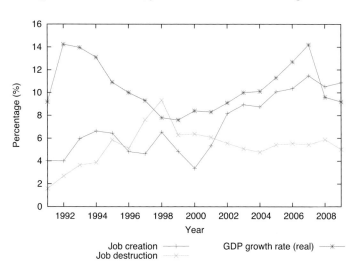

Sources: Data on job creation and destruction are obtained by the author's own calculations, while real GDP growth is from NBS (2010b) and CEInet.

5.3   Worker Reallocation

5.3.1 Categories of Worker Inflows

In this study, worker inflows in period t are measured as follows:

$$WI_{it} = NH_{it} + TI_{it} + OI_{it}, \tag{5.6}$$

where NH_{it} is the total new hires in *urban units* and includes the following categories: new hires of rural migrants, new hires of urban residents (excluding new graduates and ex-soldiers), new graduates, and ex-soldiers; TI_{it} represents the transferal of workers from other workplaces; OI_{it} represents the inflow of other workers, including other new hires in *urban units* and small firms.[2]

The annual changes in total worker inflows in each category are shown in Fig. 5.7, including a short period of increase in the early 1990s, followed by a decrease between 1993 and 2000, and then rapid and continuous growing after 2000.

Fig. 5.7 Worker inflows in urban China

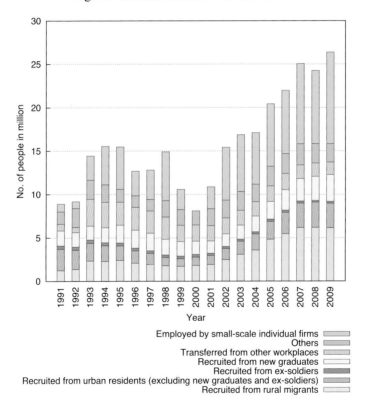

Employed by small-scale individual firms
Others
Transferred from other workplaces
Recruited from new graduates
Recruited from ex-soldiers
Recruited from urban residents (excluding new graduates and ex-soldiers)
Recruited from rural migrants

Source: Author's calculation from NBS (1992–2010a)

---

2. As details on workers in small firms are not reported, we list them as a separate group. While the number shown in Fig 5.7 is large, the actual number could be even larger, because the data include only the net increase in employment in small firms.

During the period investigated, especially after 2000, the large-scale rural–urban migration in China led to a rise in the inflow of new hires from rural migrants. As shown in Fig. 5.8, during 1991–1993, there were an increase in the new hires of rural migrants and a decrease in the new hires of urban residents. However, after 1993, the two labor groups showed the same trend. After 2001, there was a significant increase in both migrant and resident workers.

Fig. 5.8 Annual changes in new hires of rural migrants and urban residents

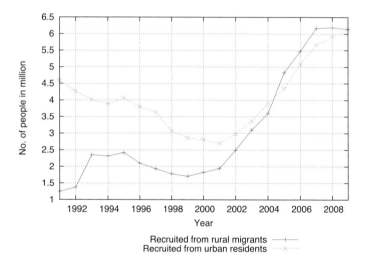

Source: Author's calculation from NBS (1992–2010a)

Further, these post-2001 increases in both migrant and resident workers were mainly caused by the expansion of private sector employment, as shown in Figs. 5.9 and 5.10. These figures illustrate that while the new hires of migrant and resident workers in the state-owned and collective sectors remained at the same level, those in the private sector increased significantly.

Fig. 5.9 New hires of rural migrants by sector

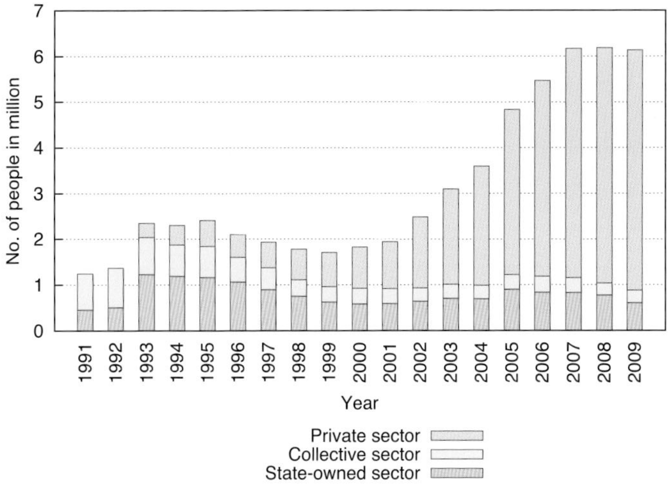

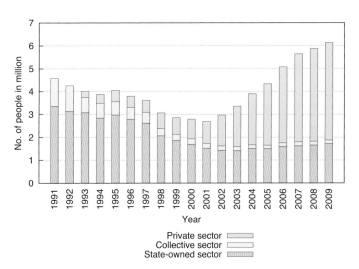

Source: Author's calculation from NBS (1992–2010a)

Fig. 5.10 New hires of urban residents by sector

Source: Author's calculation from NBS (1992–2010a)

5.3.2 Categories of Worker Outflows

Our measurement of worker outflows in period t is as follows:

$$WO_{it} = CE_{it} + FI_{it} + LA_{it} + TO_{it} + RE_{it} + OO_{it}, \qquad (5.7)$$

where CE_{it} represents contract terminations (at the initiatives of either the firm or the worker), FI_{it} represents firings, LA_{it} stands for layoffs, TO_{it} represents transfers to other workplaces, RE_{it} represents retirements, and OO_{it} denotes other worker outflows, such as the death of an employed worker.

The proportions by category are shown in Fig. 5.11. In the late 1990s, the largest share of worker outflows came from layoffs. However, starting from around 2000, layoffs decreased and contract terminations increased significantly; these became the main reason for job exits. The difference between layoffs and contract terminations is that the former are caused by politics, leading to worker retrenchment in the state-owned and collective sectors, whereas the latter are initiated by firms or workers (Fig. 5.12).

Fig. 5.11 Categories of worker outflows in urban China

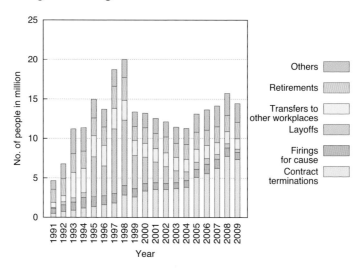

Source: Author's calculation from NBS (1992–2010a)

Fig. 5.12 Categories of worker outflows in the state-owned, collective and private sectors

(a) State-owned sector

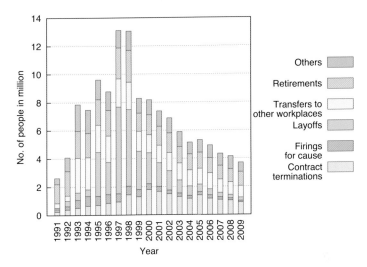

(b) Collective sector

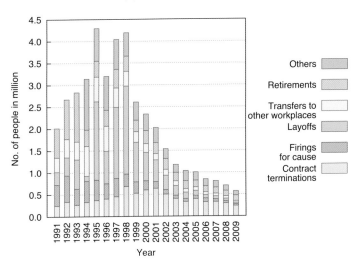

(c) Private sector

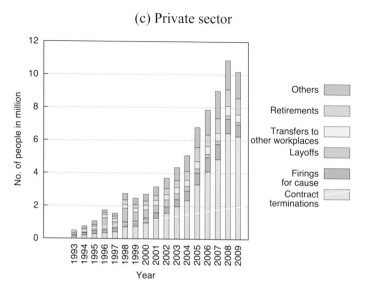

Source: Author's calculation from NBS (1992–2010a)

Fig. 5.12(c) shows that extremely frequent contract terminations occur in the private sector. When a job becomes profitless, firms terminate the contract or refuse to renew expired agreements. In particular, firms in the private-sector often enter into short-term contracts with workers to take advantage of the lower costs of employment (Han 2008). For instance, many private firms enter into one-year contracts with migrant workers so that once a job is no longer profitable, they can easily terminate the employee's contract at the end of the year at little cost.[3] Contracts can also end or be terminated when workers quit. On-the-job searches have therefore increased in China for many reasons, including unstable employment because of short-term contracts and slower wage growth in the same firm compared with earnings after changing jobs.

---

3. A firm only has to convert an employment contract into a permanent one when it has continuously employed the worker for 10 years, according to the labor laws enacted prior to 2007. New labor laws came into effect in 2008, with an additional clause: a firm that renews a contract more than twice should convert the contract into a permanent one.

5.4   Conclusions

Job and worker reallocations represent the dynamics of a labor market. This chapter examined the characteristics of job creation, job destruction and worker flows in urban China. We found that the rates of job creation and destruction were high in the late 1990s and 2000s, which resulted in vast job reallocations during that period. Moreover, job reallocations were higher than net employment growth because millions of jobs were created in the expanded private sector at the expense of diminishing positions in SOEs. Therefore, the economic reforms in China not only destroyed a great number of state jobs, but also led to large-scale job creations and reallocations both within and between industrial sectors.

Worker reallocations were even larger than job reallocations because of job-to-job worker transfers and recruitments to replace retirees. Further, there was a noteworthy change in employment inflows due to rural–urban migration, which increased fivefold from 1991 to 2009. The inflow of urban residents into employment increased, too. Although there was a decline during the retrenchment program, the inflow of residents into employment recovered starting from 2001, and the level in 1991 was surpassed in 2005. On the other hand, employment outflows were mainly caused by layoffs because of the enterprise reforms and contract terminations out of the profit-maximizing behaviors of firms.

Job and worker reallocations usually cause frictions in the labor market (Cahuc and Zylberberg 2004), lengthening the time needed for jobseekers to find suitable jobs and for job vacancies to be matched to workers. Against this background of high reallocations in the labor market in China, Chapter 6 will examine the process of matching jobseekers with job vacancies.

6

Labor Market Matching

6.1 Introduction

High job rotations and worker reallocations have increased frictions in the urban labor market of China, increasing the time necessary for a worker to find a satisfactory job and for a firm to select a suitable employee. These frictions can be captured in a matching model, which has been used widely to explore labor market issues. Matching theory provides a tool for fractional unemployment analysis and enables the modeling of the contribution of jobseekers and job vacancies to new hires in a labor market that has imperfect information (see Diamond and Maskin 1979; Blanchard et al. 1989; Pissarides 2000). In this chapter, we thus estimate matching models for the Chinese labor market and consider heterogeneous jobseekers in the matching process.

A widely used tool to analyze labor market matching is the matching function. The general form of the matching function can be represented by $M = m(U,V)$, where M is the number of job-worker matches[1] during the given time interval (flow), U is the number of unemployed urban jobseekers (stock), and V is the number of job vacancies (stock), with the conditions of $m(U,0) = m(0,V) = 0$ and $m(U,V) \leq \min(U,V)$. The matching function is assumed to be strictly increasing with respect to each argument and concave. Most studies have found it to possess a Cobb–Douglas form, namely $M = aU^{\eta_1}V^{\eta_2}$, where a represents matching efficiency, and η_1 and η_2 measure the elasticity of jobseekers and job vacancies with respect to new hires, respectively (Petrongolo and Pissarides 2001).

---

1. Theoretically and strictly speaking, matching means successful contact between jobseekers and job vacancies (Cahuc and Zylberberg 2004). In the empirical literature, however, matches are usually assumed to be equal to new hires (Petrongolo and Pissarides 2001). Therefore, in our study, we also ignore job worker contacts that do not result in employment and assume the reject rate after contact to be unrelated to job vacancies and jobseekers.

The conventional aggregate matching function is a regression of new hires on unemployed persons and vacancies. Recent studies have found that biases can arise if employed and other non-unemployed jobseekers (such as migrant jobseekers) are ignored (see Broersma and van Ours 1999; Petrongolo and Pissarides 2001; Sunde 2007), and noted that the conventional matching function is influenced by the proportion of heterogeneous jobseekers in the marketplace (Hynninen 2009). Thus, in this chapter, we include heterogeneous factors in our matching function. Moreover, because matching efficiencies are often influenced by exogenous factors, the estimated scales of the matching function enable us to examine the determinants of matching efficiencies.

Jobseekers are typically segmented according to their employment status (van Ours 1995; Hynninen 2009). In the urban labor market in China, however, rural–urban migrants are different from both employed and unemployed residents because of the strict household registration system in place. These migrants do not receive unemployment benefits because they can fall back on farm work in their native rural areas, and thus they are not officially recognized as involuntary unemployed persons if they are unable to find urban employment. They are also more likely to accept a job than permanent residents. Thus, numerous Chinese studies have divided jobseekers in urban areas into three groups: employed, unemployed and migrant workers (Knight and Song 1995; Xie 2008), and we adopt the same segmentation (the special labor market of fresh graduates is excluded). The proportion of each labor group is shown in Fig. 6.1. Furthermore, after estimating the matching function of the total labor market, we also examine the matching processes of each group as well as the competition among them.

The remainder of this chapter is organized as follows. Section 6.2 reviews previous studies of this topic, while Section 6.3 describes the data. The aggregate matching efficiency of China is obtained by nonlinear estimations in Section 6.4, which is the core part of this chapter. The matching function of each labor group is examined in Section 6.5, while Section 6.6 sheds light on the determinants of the matching efficiencies. Section 6.7 concludes.

Fig. 6.1 Proportion of each labor group in urban China
(a) Proportion of each group of jobseekers

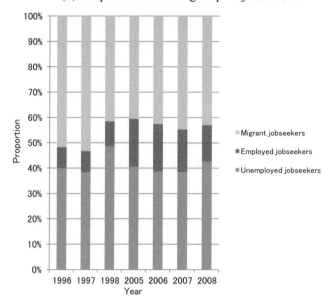

(b) Proportion of new hires from each group

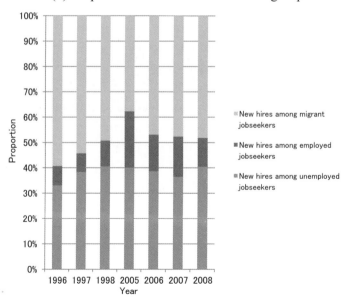

Source: NBS (1997–2009a)

6.2   Literature Review

Descriptive studies have reported the issue of mismatches between jobseekers and job vacancies and suggested this as a reason for the labor-market frictions in China (however, no studies have so far applied econometric analysis). For example, Bai and Huang (2010) reported serious mismatch problems in China, including the lack of blue-collar and gray-collar workers, the lack of senior management skills and knowledge workers, large numbers of poorly educated and physically poor unemployed jobseekers (most of whom are laid-off workers from SOEs), and a large number of fresh graduates who cannot find jobs. Similar mismatch problems were also reported in a BOJ (2008) research study on China.

Further, these mismatches have been shown to be caused by frictional rather than structural problems. Fu et al. (2010), for instance, found a significant positive correlation between industrial diversity and unemployment. Indeed, if unemployment were mainly caused by an imbalance between job vacancies and jobseekers, industrial diversity would be negatively correlated with unemployment, because industrial diversity led to more types of jobs and provided job opportunities to different types of jobseekers. Fu et al. (2010) referred to their results as "puzzling" and argued that this positive correlation was caused by the institutional barriers in urban labor markets that reduced job mobility as well as the huge number of layoffs from SOEs since the mid-1990s.

Although previous research in China has paid insufficient attention to matching theory, there have been a considerable number of studies of the empirical matching function in other countries (see Petrongolo and Pissarides 2001). Further, a few studies have involved heterogeneity in labor-market matching analysis. For instance, Burgess (1993) examined the competition caused by employed jobseekers to the unemployed, while van Ours (1995) developed two types of matching function forms to distinguish the case that employed and unemployed jobseekers search in the same pool of vacancies and the case in different pools of vacancies. Further, Broersma and van Ours (1999) used approximations for non-unemployed jobseekers (e.g. 10% of the employed workforce searches for another job). More recently, although lacking specific data on new hires by jobseeker group, Hynninen (2009) introduced such a classification into the total matching function and found significant jobseeker heterogeneity in the matching process. By using different methods, previous studies have therefore confirmed the importance of accounting for the behavior of non-unemployed jobseekers in empirical matching functions. Thus, in our study of China, we apply some of these methods to examine job–worker matching, given the heterogeneity of jobseekers in the labor market.

6.3 Data

We sourced data on job vacancies, jobseekers and new hires from approximately 30,000 public and private labor agencies across China (NBS 1997–2009a). Every region has government-operated job agencies, while some also have private job agencies. Those who register with job agencies include not only unemployed jobseekers but also rural–urban migrants and employed jobseekers. The unemployed population includes both registered unemployed persons and laid-off workers.

The datasets complied by job agencies provide information on the number of jobseekers by group, the flow of new hires from each group, and job vacancies. The quarterly report of the Chinese labor market covers job agencies located in 100 large cities nationwide, while the annual report includes all official and private job agencies across China. Therefore, although not all jobseekers are registered with job agencies, job-agency data form the most complete macro dataset on job searches in China, and using these data has been a common method in related studies (e.g., Hynninen 2009; Coles and Smith 1996; Kano and Ohta 2005). In particular, the job-agency data of China have an advantage that new hires, jobseekers, and job vacancies refer to the same pool of workers and jobs, which is rarely the case in other countries (see Petrongolo and Pissarides 2001).

Based on the foregoing, we use provincial data from the annual report of the Chinese labor market. The period covered is 1996–2008 for a cross-section of 29 Chinese provinces.[2] Further, we use the number of job agencies per employment scale, je_{it} , as the index of job-search services. je_{it} is calculated from JE_{it} / E_{it}, where JE_{it} is the total number of job agencies and E_{it} stands for employment. Other macro data come from NBS (1997–2009b), taken directly or with several adjustments. For instance, for data on productivity, we use labor productivity data, which are the rates

---

2. Hong Kong, Macau, Xinjiang, Tibet and Taiwan are excluded.

of output per worker in urban areas. The data on productivity growth are recorded as annual differences in productivity. Productivity data are thus real figures after the price-index adjustment. The data descriptions and summary statistics are presented in Table 6.1.

Table 6.1 Data description and summary statistics for
the labor market matching analysis

Var.	Definition	Data description	Mean	Std. Dev.	Obs.
S_{it}	Job seekers	Number of job seekers in job agencies (10,000 persons)	100.00	121.28	376
M_{it}	New hires	Number of annual new hires in job agencies (10,000 persons)	53.32	57.54	376
U_{it}	Unemployed job seekers	Number of unemployed job seekers in job agencies (10,000 persons)	43.40	51.01	372
S_{it}^{e}	Employed job seekers	Number of employed job seekers in job agencies (10,000 persons)	18.67	33.91	186
S_{it}^{m}	Migrant job seekers	Number of migrant job seekers in job agencies (10,000 persons)	49.17	75.16	197
V_{it}	Job vacancies	Number of vacant jobs in job agencies (10,000 persons)	96.99	154.02	376
H_{it}^{u}	New hires from unemployed job seekers	Number of annual new hires from unemployed workers in job agencies (10,000 persons)	23.15	23.76	368
H_{it}^{m}	New hires from migrant job seekers	Number of annual new hires from migrant job seekers in job agencies (10,000 persons)	29.28	35.10	195
λ_{it}	Job destruction rate	The ratio of annual inflows into registered unemployment and layoff to total employment	0.06	0.04	174
θ_{it}	Market tightness	$\theta = V / (U + \phi S^{e} + \varphi S^{m})$	0.47	0.14	187
JE_{it}	Job search service	Number of job agencies	1115.31	716.51	375
P_{it}	Productivity	Annual production per worker (labor productivity; *yuan*)	33966.34	19280.83	375

Sources: NBS 1997–2009a, NBS 1997–2009b.

6.4   Aggregate Matching Function in China

We first estimate an aggregate matching function of the total labor market in order to describe the job–worker matching process in China. The conventional aggregate matching function is estimated as $M = aU^{\alpha}V^{\beta}$, where M represents new hires from the unemployed population, U stands for unemployed jobseekers, and V represents total notified job vacancies (Pissarides 2000, chap. 1). It must be noted that estimates can be biased if there are jobseekers other than unemployed persons. Based on this fact, Pissarides (2000, chap. 4) suggested a matching function of $m(U + E^{s}, V)$ when unemployed workers, U, and employed workers, E^{s}, apply to the same kinds of jobs, implying that congestion externalities flow bidirectionally between both groups of workers. Further, considering the heterogeneities of jobseekers in China, and following the approach of van Ours (1995), we set the following form:

$$M = a(U + \phi S^{e} + \varphi S^{m})^{\eta_1} V^{\eta_2}, \tag{6.1}$$

where M represents total new hires, a stands for matching efficiency (which varies by year and region), S^{e} is the number of employed urban jobseekers, S^{m} is the number of migrant jobseekers, ϕ and φ are the heterogeneities of the three labor groups in the matching process, and η_1 and η_2 stand for the elasticity of jobseekers and job vacancies with respect to new hires, respectively.

This estimation is complicated because of a log-nonlinear form and many unknown parameters. As most of the empirical studies carried out in other countries have found the matching function to be homogeneous of degree 1 (Petrongolo and Pissarides 2001), we first examine whether the hypothesis that $\eta_1 + \eta_2 = 1$ is supported by a reduced-form estimation that introduces all the possible factors influencing new matches. The estimation result is reported in Appendix 6A. Since the null hypothesis that $\eta_1 + \eta_2 = 1$ is not rejected, we assume the matching function of the entire labor market to be homogeneous of degree 1. The estimation equation is thus given as follows:

$$\ln M_{it} = \eta \ln(U_{it} + \phi S^{e}_{it} + \varphi S^{m}_{it}) + (1 - \eta) \ln V_{it} + a_{i} + a_{t} + \varepsilon_{it}, \tag{6.2}$$

where a_i and a_t denote the fixed effects of the cross-sections and time series respectively, $\exp(a_i + a_t) = a_{it}$, η, ϕ, φ are the estimated coefficients, t stands for seven years, and i represents 28 provinces (we exclude the Qinghai province because the number of employed jobseekers is reported as zero, which is unlikely).

We use two estimation methods. The first is a panel nonlinear least squares estimation method denoted as Model (1). We also use a second method to avoid the biases that could arise from possible correlations between the independent variables and residuals; we denote this as Model (2). The endogenous variables being instrumented are S_{it}^e, S_{it}^m and V_{it} and the instruments are $S_{i,t-1}^e$, $S_{i,t-1}^m$ and $V_{i,t-1}$. Both results successfully converge after several iterations. Although our dataset spans from 1996 to 2008, the numbers of migrant and urban employed jobseekers are aggregated in the period 2000–2004. Hence, the estimation results of Models (1) and (2) cover seven years, from 1996 to 1998 and from 2005 to 2008.

Moreover, we note that the values of the estimates of ϕ and φ do not seem to differ significantly and thus we run the Wald test to examine whether $\phi = \varphi$. The result indicates that the null hypothesis of $\phi = \varphi$ cannot be rejected. We therefore assume that $\phi = \varphi$ and add this restriction into our models, thereby allowing us to use all the information from the 13-year period between 1996 and 2008. Using estimation methods similar to those applied to Models (1) and (2), results are obtained from Models (3) and (4), as reported in Table 6.2.

We obtain rather significant estimates, which are consistent with matching theory. Jobseekers and job vacancies contribute significantly to new hires, following a Cobb–Douglas function form, as they do in most other countries. Further, $\phi > 1$ and $\varphi > 1$ indicate that the contributions of migrant and employed jobseekers to new hires are greater than those of unemployed jobseekers. This higher contribution of employed jobseekers could arise from their access to more job-search information through work-related networks; moreover, migrants can apply for more vacant jobs and accept the offered wages more easily because of their much lower reservation wage. The reservation wage of migrants is low because of the income gap between urban and rural areas: even the lowest wage in urban areas is higher than the incomes of most farmers. On the contrary, the reservation wage of unemployed urban residents is high because of government subsidies and unemployment benefits. Because local

Table 6.2 Estimation results of the aggregate matching models

	Matching models			
	Model (1)	Model (2)	Model (3)	Model (4)
	Nonlinear	Nonlinear	Nonlinear	Nonlinear
	LS	2SLS	LS	2SLS
η	0.52	0.80	0.69	0.81
	[2.71]*	[5.89]***	[7.11]***	[4.13]***
	[9.34]***	[5.42]***	[16.97]***	[7.67]***
ϕ	1.52	2.08	1.71	2.06
	[1.35]	[1.56]	[2.93]**	[0.48]
	[2.51]*	[2.07]**	[6.55]***	[1.48]
φ	1.89	2.93	1.71	2.06
	[2.75]*	[1.55]	[2.93]**	[0.48]
	[3.05]**	[1.07]	[6.55]***	[1.48]
Const.	−0.51	−0.86	−0.70	−0.93
	[−2.19]*	[−2.06] *	[−3.12]**	[−0.61]
	[−3.25]***	[−1.55]	[−6.97]***	[−1.75]*
a_i	Yes	Yes	Yes	Yes
a_t	Yes	Yes	Yes	Yes
R-squared	0.97	0.99	0.96	0.96
Adj. R-squared	0.96	0.98	0.95	0.95
p-value of $H_0 : \phi = \varphi$	0.671	0.702	—	—
Restriction of $\phi = \varphi$	No	No	Yes	Yes
N	187	106	372	369
Period	(1996–1998, 2005–2008)	(1998, 2005–2008)	(1996– 2008)	(1996– 2008)

Notes:

(1) The t-statistics and z-statistics are given in parentheses. Below every estimate, the first line presents either the t-statistics or the z-statistics based on the standard errors clustered at the provincial level; for comparison, the second line is based on ordinary standard errors.

(2) In model (1), the period does not include 1999–2004 owing to data limitations.

(3) In model (2), the period does not include 1996–1997 and 1999–2004 owing to data limitations.

(4) *p < 0.1, **p < 0.05, ***p < 0.01

governments provide unemployed residents, especially those laid off from SOEs, with basic living conditions, they are able to spend more time searching for the most suitable jobs.

Further, we examine the changes in job–worker matching efficiency during the sample period. Because matching efficiency is defined as $a_{it} = \exp(a_i + a_t)$, its time changes comprise the period effects of $\exp a_t$. The estimated changes in $\exp a_t$, according to the two estimation methods, are displayed in Fig. 6.2.

Fig. 6.2 shows that the matching efficiency of the entire labor market experienced a sharp decline during 1996–2008. As discussed in Chapter 5, China experienced large-scale job and worker reallocations in the late 1990s and early 2000s. High job and worker mobility usually leads to serious labor market frictions, which lowers the efficiency of job–worker matching (Cahuc and Zylberberg 2004). Some qualitative studies have pointed out that labor market frictions are serious in China (e.g., Wang 2010; Dai 2010; Dong 2010) and these caused a steep decline in matching efficiency during the period investigated. Furthermore, matching efficiency can be improved through the development of job-search services. However, although the number of job agencies increased during this period, the ratio of agencies to the expanding employment scale actually decreased. Moreover, productivity growth may have caused a skill mismatch between jobseekers and job vacancies. We will discuss these issues quantitatively in Section 6.6.

Fig. 6.2 Changes in the total matching efficiency of China's labor market
(a) Result of Model (1)

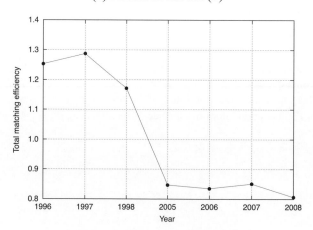

(b) Result of Model (2)

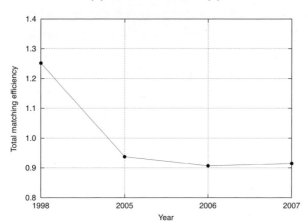

(c) Result of Model (3)

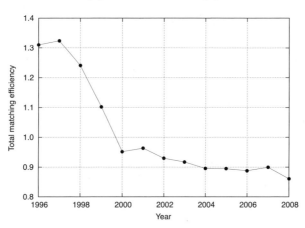

(d) Result of Model (4)

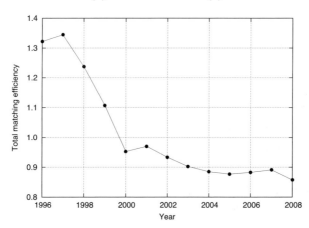

Source: Author's estimation.

The total matching function provides the aggregate matching efficiency of the entire labor market. Although it is possible to obtain the detailed matching efficiency of each labor group, the aggregate matching efficiency is more important for firms' job creation decisions, because it provides information on the entire labor market. Nevertheless, the separate matching functions of each jobseeker group might have similar characteristics to the aggregate matching function, which we will examine in Section 6.5.

6.5   Matching Function of Each Jobseeker Group

The dataset described in Section 6.3 provides information on the new hires sourced from each labor group. Note that job vacancies cannot be divided separately because firms are not able to predict which labor group will be matched when they post job vacancies. All three labor groups look for jobs in the same job vacancy pool, and the possible competition among them can thus cause congestion. Therefore, we not only consider the contributions of jobseekers and job vacancies to the matching result, but also introduce the variables of congestion externalities, which are important factors in the matching process. The terms of these congestion externalities are based on the findings of Ibourk et al. (2004). The general matching functions for each jobseeker group are given as:

$$H^u = a_u U^{\alpha_u} EUV^{\beta_u}, \tag{6.3}$$

$$H^e = a_e (S^e)^{\alpha_e} EEV^{\beta_e}, \tag{6.4}$$

$$H^m = a_m (S^m)^{\alpha_m} EMV^{\beta_m}, \tag{6.5}$$

where H^u, H^e and H^m represent new hires from unemployed, employed and urban–rural migrant jobseekers respectively, and U, S^e and S^m represent unemployed, employed and rural–urban migrant jobseekers respectively. Further, a_u, a_e and a_m are the matching efficiencies of unemployed, employed and migrant jobseekers respectively. Finally, EUV, EEV and EMV are the efficient job vacancies for unemployed, employed and migrant jobseekers respectively:

$$EUV = V - \lambda^{ue} V \frac{S^e}{S} - \lambda^{um} V \frac{S^m}{S}, \tag{6.6}$$

$$EEV = V - \lambda^{eu}V\frac{U}{S} - \lambda^{em}V\frac{S^m}{S}, \tag{6.7}$$

$$EMV = V - \lambda^{mu}V\frac{U}{S} - \lambda^{me}V\frac{S^e}{S}, \tag{6.8}$$

where λ is significantly positive if the other two groups of jobseekers cause congestion in job vacancies. We take logarithms of these three general matching functions and use the Taylor approximation to assume that

$$\ln(1 - \lambda^{ue}\frac{S^e}{S} - \lambda^{um}\frac{S^m}{S}) \approx -\lambda^{ue}\frac{S^e}{S} - \lambda^{um}\frac{S^m}{S}, \tag{6.9}$$

$$\ln(1 - \lambda^{eu}\frac{U}{S} - \lambda^{em}\frac{S^m}{S}) \approx -\lambda^{eu}\frac{U}{S} - \lambda^{em}\frac{S^m}{S}, \tag{6.10}$$

$$\ln(1 - \lambda^{mu}\frac{U}{S} - \lambda^{me}\frac{S^e}{S}) \approx -\lambda^{mu}\frac{U}{S} - \lambda^{me}\frac{S^e}{S}, \tag{6.11}$$

in EUV, EEV and EMV, respectively. Accordingly, the estimation equation of each labor group is given as follows:

$$\ln H_{it}^u = \alpha_u \ln U_{it} + \beta_u \ln V_{it} - \lambda^{ue}\frac{S_{it}^e}{S_{it}} - \lambda^{um}\frac{S_{it}^m}{S_{it}} + a_i^u + a_t^u + \varepsilon_{it}^u, \tag{6.12}$$

$$\ln H_{it}^e = \alpha_e \ln S_{it}^e + \beta_e \ln V_{it} - \lambda^{eu}\frac{U_{it}}{S_{it}} - \lambda^{em}\frac{S_{it}^m}{S_{it}} + a_i^e + a_t^e + \varepsilon_{it}^e, \tag{6.13}$$

$$\ln H_{it}^m = \alpha_m \ln S_{it}^m + \beta_m \ln V_{it} - \lambda^{mu}\frac{U_{it}}{S_{it}} - \lambda^{me}\frac{S_{it}^e}{S_{it}} + a_i^m + a_t^m + \varepsilon_{it}^m, \tag{6.14}$$

where S_{it} is the total number of jobseekers, and U_{it}/S_{it}, S_{it}^e/S_{it} and S_{it}^m/S_{it} can be explained as the indices of congestion externalities from the other groups of jobseekers. The matching efficiencies a_{it}^u, a_{it}^e and a_{it}^m are then defined as $a_{it}^u = \exp(a_i^u + a_t^u)$, $a_{it}^e = \exp(a_i^e + a_t^e)$ and $a_{it}^m = \exp(a_i^m + a_t^m)$, respectively.

For the sake of endogeneity and correlation among the residuals, we apply 3SLS analysis to our estimation, with a specification for both the cross-section fixed and the period fixed effects.[3] We also use other estimation methods for comparison purposes (see Table 6.3). We therefore obtain the econometric model of the matching function of each labor group as follows:

$$\ln H_{it}^{u} = 0.53\ln U_{it} + 0.23\ln V_{it} + 0.51\frac{S_{it}^{e}}{S_{it}} + 0.13\frac{S_{it}^{m}}{S_{it}} + a_{i}^{u} + a_{t}^{u} + \varepsilon_{it}^{u}, \quad (6.15)$$

$$(5.6)^{***} \qquad (2.1)^{**} \qquad (1.6) \qquad (0.5) \qquad \text{Adj. R} = 0.95$$

$$\ln H_{it}^{e} = 0.48\ln S_{it}^{e} + 0.64\ln V_{it} - 1.67\frac{U_{it}}{S_{it}} - 1.49\frac{S_{it}^{m}}{S_{it}} + a_{i}^{e} + a_{t}^{e} + \varepsilon_{it}^{e}, \quad (6.16)$$

$$(5.4)^{***} \qquad (3.5)^{***} \qquad (-2.1)^{*} \qquad (-1.7)^{**} \quad \text{Adj. R} = 0.89$$

$$\ln H_{it}^{m} = 0.44\ln S_{it}^{m} + 0.42\ln V_{it} - 1.04\frac{U_{it}}{S_{it}} - 0.43\frac{S_{it}^{e}}{S_{it}} + a_{i}^{m} + a_{t}^{m} + \varepsilon_{it}^{m}, \quad (6.17)$$

$$(2.8)^{***} \qquad (2.6)^{***} \qquad (-1.9)^{*} \qquad (-1.0) \qquad \text{Adj. R} = 0.92$$

The presented results indicate that for new matches from unemployed workers, both unemployed jobseekers and job vacancies contribute to the outcomes significantly, while the factor of congestion externalities from the other groups of jobseekers is not significant.

The result that an increase in non-unemployed jobseekers does not influence the job searches of unemployed jobseekers is slightly surprising. This finding might be explained by local policy measures, which usually favor the city's own unemployed residents over other jobseekers. For instance, local enterprises receive tax relief for three years if they recruit a particular number of laid-off resident workers (MOF 2002). A similar result is reported in Knight and Song (2005).

---

3. We examine the endogeneity problem using the Durbin and Wu–Hausman tests. The null hypothesis that the variable under consideration can be treated as exogenous is rejected in Equation (6.13) but not so in Equations (6.12) and (6.14). Therefore, we estimate a 3SLS specification with instruments in all equations. The relevance and exogeneity of the instruments are also examined.

Table 6.3 Estimation results of the matching function of each labor group

(a) Dep. Var.: $\ln H_{it}^{u}$

Indep. Var.	Model	Comparison			
	3SLS	2SLS	SUR	OLS	2SLS'
$\ln U_{it}$	0.53	0.53	0.50	0.48	0.45
	[5.58]***	[5.57]***	[8.85]***	[7.73]***	[4.73]***
$\ln V_{it}$	0.23	0.23	0.30	0.30	0.31
	[2.06]**	[2.07]**	[6.09]***	[5.44]***	[3.69]***
S_{it}^{m} / S_{it}	0.13	0.13	0.03	−0.04	−
	[0.47]	[0.46]	[0.14]	[−0.20]	−
S_{it}^{e} / S_{it}	0.51	0.51	0.38	0.33	−
	[1.60]	[1.68]*	[1.78]*	[1.40]	−
Year dummy	Yes	Yes	Yes	Yes	Yes
Regional dummy	Yes	Yes	Yes	Yes	Yes
R	0.97	0.97	1.00	0.97	0.97
Adj. R	0.95	0.96	0.98	0.96	0.96
N	178	178	174	182	178

Instrumental variables: $\ln U_{it}$, $\ln V_{it}$; Instruments: $\ln S_{it}$, $\ln S_{it}^{e}$, $\ln S_{it}^{m}$

(b) Dep. Var.: $\ln H_{it}^{e}$

Indep. Var.	Model	Comparison			
	3SLS	2SLS	SUR	OLS	2SLS'
$\ln S_{it}^{e}$	0.48	0.49	0.56	0.49	0.63
	[5.38]***	[5.38]***	[7.07]***	[5.51]***	[14.07]***
$\ln V_{it}$	0.64	0.64	0.52	0.63	0.55
	[3.54]***	[3.53]***	[5.01]***	[5.12]***	[3.96]***
U_{it} / S_{it}	−1.67	−1.66	−1.30	−1.66	−
	[−1.66]*	[−2.07]**	[−1.75]*	[−1.89]*	−

Table 6.3 (continued)

Indep. Var.	3SLS	2SLS	SUR	OLS	2SLS'
S_{it}^m / S_{it}	−1.49	−1.49	−1.48	−1.47	–
	[−2.08]**	[−1.65]*	[−1.92]*	[−1.63]	–
Year dummy	Yes	Yes	Yes	Yes	Yes
Regional dummy	Yes	Yes	Yes	Yes	Yes
R	0.91	0.91	0.95	0.91	0.91
Adj. R	0.89	0.88	0.91	0.88	0.88
N	183	183	174	183	183

Instrumental variables: $\ln V_{it}$; Instruments: $\ln S_{it}$, $\ln S_{it}^m$, $\ln U_{it}$

(c) Dep. Var.: $\ln H_{it}^m$

	Model	Comparison			
Indep. Var.	3SLS	2SLS	SUR	OLS	2SLS'
$\ln S_{it}^m$	0.44	0.44	0.52	0.52	0.51
	[2.84]***	[2.84]***	[7.79]***	[7.07]***	[4.30]***
$\ln V_{it}$	0.42	0.42	0.42	0.40	0.45
	[2.64]***	[2.64]***	[6.12]***	[5.23]***	[2.77]***
U_{it} / S_{it}	−1.04	−1.04	−0.58	−0.74	–
	[−1.89]*	[−1.89]*	[−1.64]*	[−1.91]*	–
S_{it}^e / S_{it}	0.43	−0.43	0.00	−0.24	–
	[0.96]	[−0.96]	[0.01]	[−0.70]	–
Year dummy	Yes	Yes	Yes	Yes	Yes
Regional dummy	Yes	Yes	Yes	Yes	Yes
R	0.94	0.94	1.00	0.94	0.94
Adj. R	0.92	0.93	0.98	0.93	0.92
N	180	180	174	184	180

Instrumented variables: $\ln S_{it}^m$, $\ln V_{it}$; Instruments: $\ln S_{it}$, $\ln S_{it}^e$, $\ln U_{it}$

Note: *p < 0.1, **p < 0.05, ***p < 0.01.

Furthermore, the indices of annual changes in matching efficiencies are displayed in Fig. 6.3, which shows that the matching efficiencies of all three jobseeker groups generally decreased in the late 1990s. This finding is consistent with the results of the gross matching efficiency of the total labor market.

Fig. 6.3 Changes in the matching efficiencies of the three jobseeker groups
(a) Unemployed jobseekers

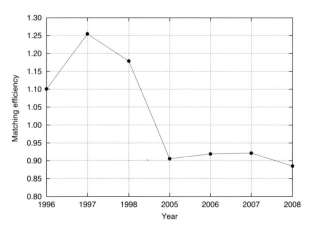

(b) Employed jobseekers

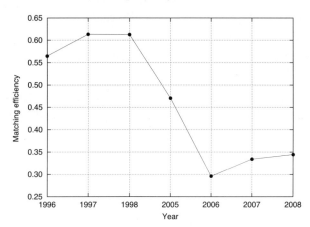

(c) Migrant jobseekers

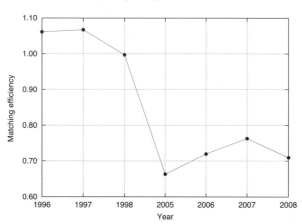

Source: Author's estimation.

6.6   Determinants of Matching Efficiency

Although it is recognized that matching efficiency plays an important role in the matching process, no existing theoretical framework can be used to determine matching efficiency, and previous studies have often examined potential determinants based on real-life situations (see Destefanis and Fonseca 2007). In China's case, matching efficiency can also be determined by factors such as job-search services, and it can also have some exogenous shocks. We thus consider both of these factors in our study and assume that matching efficiency comprises both endogenous and exogenous factors in China.

According to Petrongolo and Pissarides (2001), technological advances such as the computerization of employment offices and online job advertising, as well as increase in government subsidies for matching, all serve as endogenous factors. Therefore, we assume that, in China, the endogenous part a^{en} is determined by the job-search services provided by job agencies je, the job destruction rate λ, and productivity changes Δp, where Δp is the index of changes in firm demand for worker skills. Since frictions often arise from mismatches between certain job vacancies and worker skills (Cahuc and Zylberberg 2004, 518), the quicker the level of job productivity changes, the more difficult it is for workers to find suitable jobs and for the current skills of jobseekers to be suitably matched to the new demands made by firms.

The exogenous shock of a is assumed to be a^{ex}. An important cause of this shock was the high degree of worker reallocation during the sample period. A large number of the workers who lost their jobs in SOEs had to look for work in the private sector, and such worker mobility increased frictional unemployment (Cahuc and Zylberberg 2004). Note that our model separates the effects of worker reallocation from those of job destruction, because higher worker reallocation unambiguously increases frictions in the labor market, whereas job destruction can either increase or decrease matching efficiency, depending on whether the destroyed jobs are more easily matched to jobseekers. As a result, the determination equations of the two matching efficiencies are given as follows:

$$a = a^{en}(je, \Delta p, \lambda) + a^{ex}, \tag{6.18}$$

$$a^u = a_u^{en}(je, \Delta p, \lambda) + a_u^{ex}, \tag{6.19}$$

$$a^e = a_e^{en}(je, \Delta p, \lambda) + a_e^{ex}, \tag{6.20}$$

$$a^m = a_m^{en}(je, \Delta p, \lambda) + a_m^{ex}, \tag{6.21}$$

where a^{ex} represents the residuals of the estimation.

As noted in Section 6.5, the values of a, a^u, a^e and a^m were obtained from $a_{it} = \exp(a_i + a_t)$, $a_{it}^u = \exp(a_i^u + a_t^u)$, $a_{it}^e = \exp(a_i^e + a_t^e)$ and $a_{it}^m = \exp(a_i^m + a_t^m)$. We thus choose to present the results derived from Model (2) for the remainder of this analysis. As reported in Table 6.4, job-search services je have significant positive effects on all matching efficiencies. This finding indicates that local job-search services in China contribute efficiently to job–worker matching. Conversely, the fewer job-search services available, the harder it is for jobseekers to be matched to job vacancies.

Table 6.4 Estimation results of the determinants of the matching efficiencies

	a_{it}	a_{it}^{u}	a_{it}^{e}	a_{it}^{m}
Indep. Var.				
je_{it}	0.05	0.14	0.14	0.15
	[2.93]***	[1.78]*	[3.67]***	[3.18]***
Δp_{it}	-4.00×10^{-6}	-8.07×10^{-5}	-4.39×10^{-5}	-2.43×10^{-5}
	[−1.13]	[−5.38]***	[−6.04]***	[−2.85]***
λ_{it}	0.73	−1.21	0.38	0.62
	[3.34]***	[−1.14]	[0.73]	[1.03]
Const.	0.3	0.61	0.53	0.84
	[7.89]***	[3.15]***	[5.73]***	[7.65]***
Regional dummy	Yes	Yes	Yes	Yes
R	0.8	0.62	0.67	0.79
Adj. R	0.72	0.54	0.6	0.74
N	116	172	172	172

Note: *$p < 0.1$, **$p < 0.05$, ***$p < 0.01$

Further, productivity growth, Δp, has a significant negative effect on a^{u}, which indicates that the matching efficiency of unemployed workers is lower in those regions that have higher productivity growth. There could also be skill mismatches between unemployed workers and job vacancies. The large number of unemployed urban workers laid off from inefficient SOEs may be used to low productivity and high reservation wages, making it difficult for them to meet the skill demands of the newly created jobs in the private sector, which involve keen competition in the market economy and generally pay market-clearing wages. Moreover, productivity growth, Δp, also has significant negative effects on a^{e} and a^{m}, although to a lower degree than those on a^{u}. This finding indicates that productivity growth may also reduce the matching efficiencies of employed and migrant jobseekers by exacerbating skill mismatches.

In addition, these results indicate that job destruction may decrease the matching efficiencies of unemployed workers and increase those of employed and migrant jobseekers, although the estimation values are less significant. The reason for this situation could be that most of the jobs destroyed in the enterprise reforms were those in SOEs, which were easier to match with unemployed residents compared with jobs in private enterprises. Thus, the lower the proportion of SOEs jobs to total jobs, the more difficult it is for unemployed residents to find new jobs. On the contrary, employed jobseekers would rather search for new jobs that require high efficiency, which exist not only in SOEs but also in private enterprises. Moreover, migrant jobseekers are often discriminated against when applying for positions in SOEs and thus most of them prefer to search for jobs in other enterprises. Therefore, the destruction of jobs in SOEs might provide employed and migrant jobseekers with more suitable jobs in other enterprises. Further, note that job destruction has a significant positive effect on the matching efficiency of the total labor market, a_{it}, which indicates that the positive effects of job destruction on the matching efficiencies of employed and migrant jobseekers could be much stronger than the negative effects on the matching efficiencies of unemployed workers.

Finally, in addition to the three factors described above, considerable exogenous shocks also arise from the frictions in the labor market. Thus, in summary, increasing frictions, underdeveloped job-search services and productivity growth jointly lead to a decline in matching efficiency in China's labor market.

6.7 Conclusions

In this chapter, we analyzed the matching process between job vacancies and jobseekers by considering three groups of heterogeneous jobseekers under a matching function framework. We found that the matching process in China's labor market strongly supports the assumptions of matching theory, such as a strict increase with respect to each argument and concave function, as well as constant returns to scale. Further, the estimates of heterogeneity indices between unemployed jobseekers and non-unemployed job seekers were rather significant, indicating that employed jobseekers and migrant jobseekers performed better in the matching process than unemployed job seekers.

Another important finding was that the matching efficiency of China's labor market declined considerably during the period 1996–2008 owing to the shocks brought about by the economic reforms, which led to high job and worker reallocations and increased market frictions. Job-search services and productivity growth were also found to be important determinants.

We also estimated the matching function of each of the three labor groups and found that the matching efficiencies of all groups experienced a similar trend, namely a large decline throughout the sample period. Further, the determinants of job-search services and productivity growth have similar effects among the three labor groups, namely a positive effect of job-search services and a negative effect of productivity growth. By contrast, the effects of job destruction on their matching efficiencies differ, showing a negative effect on the new hires of unemployed resident jobseekers and a positive effect on the new hires of both employed and migrant jobseekers.

A greater number of job–worker matches makes a significant contribution to labor market outcomes and reduces the unemployment rate. China's matching process has been influenced by the decline in matching efficiency, as described in this chapter. However, as indicated by the matching function, more newly created jobs could increase the number of matches. In Chapter 7, we will shed further light on the determinants of job creation in urban China.

Appendix 6A   Tests of the Constant Returns to Scale in the Aggregate Matching Function

The constant returns to scale in the aggregate matching function, $\eta_1 + \eta_2 = 1$, are tested by a reduced-form estimation, as follows:

$$\ln M_{it} = \eta_1 \ln(U_{it} + \phi S_{it}^e + \varphi S_{it}^m) + \eta_2 \ln V_{it} + \beta_m^p \Delta p_{it}$$
$$+ \beta_m^{je} je_{it} + \beta_m^E E_{it} + \beta_m^\lambda \lambda_{it} + \beta_m^{r\lambda}(r_{it} + \lambda_{it})$$
$$+ c_i + c_t + \varepsilon_{it}. \qquad (6.22)$$

The results are reported in Table 6.5.

Table 6.5 indicates that the null hypothesis that $\eta_1 + \eta_2 = 1$ cannot be rejected. Hence, it is appropriate to assume the matching function of the entire labor market to be homogeneous of degree 1.

Table 6.5 Results of the tests of constant returns to scale

	Model 1	Model 2	Model 3
η_1	0.4284	0.46704	0.45395
	[6.91]***	[7.72]***	[7.27]***
η_2	0.49662	0.46348	0.48449
	[8.52]***	[8.12]***	[8.32]***
ϕ	2.30882	1.54356	2.29012
	[1.95]*	[1.94]*	[2.05]**
φ	2.6038	2.77698	2.74731
	[2.06]**	[2.40]**	[2.17]**
β_m^p	−0.00004	−0.00002	−0.00004
	[−3.19]***	[−1.20]	[−3.23]***
β_m^{je}	0.08076	0.09778	0.07339
	[1.78]*	[2.17]**	[1.59]
β_m^E	−0.00028	−0.00027	−0.00023
	[−3.24]***	[−3.18]***	[−2.54]**
β_m^λ	—	0.4394	0.37511
	—	[0.82]	[0.68]
$\beta_m^{r\lambda}$	—	—	−1.0659
	—	—	[−2.14]**
Const.	−0.32691	−0.1487	−0.37598
	[0.14]	[−1.48]	[−0.67]
p-value	**0.156**	**0.159**	**0.222**
$(H_0 : \eta_1 + \eta_2 = 1)$			
R	0.971	0.973	0.972
Adj. R	0.962	0.964	0.962
N	171	171	171

Note: *p < 0.1, **p < 0.05, ***p < 0.01

7

Determinants of Job Creation in China

7.1 Introduction

The process of job creation under China's planned economy before 1978 was managed by the government rather than being determined by market forces. The market economy in China began to develop in the early 1980s, since which job creation has greatly expanded (see the discussion in Chapter 5). In this chapter, we thus examine the factors that determine job creation in China based on the job creation model, a key component of search and matching theory.

Few previous studies have explored the determinants of job creation in China. While some have paid attention to employment growth (e.g., Yang 2008), we have already explained the difference between employment growth and job creation in Chapter 5. In the study presented by Deng et al. (2005), job creation in China is defined as employment increases by a firm starting up or expanding, which is also a common method in the calculation of job creation in other countries (see Davis and Haltiwanger 1996). However, as pointed out by Davis and Haltiwanger (1996), vacant jobs that do not lead to employment are ignored by this method. Our study in Chapter 5 also ignored such vacant jobs, and thus these methods paint only a general picture of job creation in China, making them unsuitable for econometric analysis. Hence, in this chapter, we consider both the jobs that have been filled by employment and the job vacancies that have not yet been matched to suitable workers.

Job creation relies on firm behavior in a market-driven economy. First, firms create more jobs when productivity increases, because higher productivity leads to more profit when creating jobs. Second, job destruction shocks discourage firms from job creation. As Fig. 5.6 shows, job creation changes in China are generally opposite to changes in job destruction, indicating the contrasting effects of job destruction and job creation. When there is a high degree of job destruction, a filled position, which has cost the firm search and hiring expenses, will disappear and become profitless at a higher rate, thus discouraging a firm's job creation behavior. Moreover, job creation could also be influenced by increased labor-market frictions, which may make it difficult for a vacant job to be matched to a worker, thereby leading firms to create fewer vacancies in the first place.

In this chapter, we adopt search theory in order to examine job creation in China. We deploy an index of job creation, θ, which indicates the number of jobs created in response to per unit of jobseekers. This is defined as the ratio of the number of job vacancies to the total number of jobseekers, namely θ, denoted as $\theta \equiv V / S$, where V is the number of job vacancies and S is the number of jobseekers. Note that θ is also an appropriate measure of *market tightness*, which is the ratio of job vacancies to jobseekers in the entire labor market. Therefore, θ denotes both the job creation index and market tightness in the presented model (Pissarides 2000).

Firms create the optimal number of jobs that maximizes their profits by observing product factors, the economic environment, labor market frictions, etc. Further, the endogenous wage level is also considered in this model. Unlike classical theory, here wage is determined decentrally by the firm and workers, which share the returns from employment according to a generalized Nash bargaining solution, the factors of which are related to productivity, bargaining power, market tightness, etc.

The remainder of this chapter is arranged as follows. Section 7.2 describes the theoretical model, based on which Section 7.3 constructs an estimation model and runs regressions using the 3SLS approach with coefficient constraints. Section 7.4 discusses the estimation results and presents our findings, while Section 7.5 concludes.

7.2   Model

For the theoretical background of job creation and wage determination, we employ the model of Pissarides (2000, chap. 1), as described in the following subsections.

7.2.1 Determination of Job Creation

For a given number of jobseekers, the number of job vacancies posted by firms is determined by the firms' profit maximization plans. The index of job creation, which is the ratio of job vacancies to jobseekers, θ, is defined by $\theta \equiv V /(U + \phi S^e + \varphi S^m)$. Moreover, the job creation condition is determined by a firm's expected profit from a vacant job, V', the expected profit from an occupied job, J, and the zero-profit condition.

The present discounted value of the expected profit from a vacant job, V', satisfies the Bellman equation, which is given as follows:

$$rV' = -pc + q(\theta)(J - V'), \tag{7.1}$$

where r denotes the interest rate, p is the value of a job's output, and pc is the hiring cost for a job with productivity p. The left-hand side of the equation denotes the capital cost of the asset of the vacant job created by the firm, which equals the rate of return on the asset shown on the right-hand side. The vacant job costs pc per unit of time, and it changes its state (to an occupied job) according to a Poisson process at a rate $q(\theta)$, where $q(\theta) = M / V$. Using the total aggregate matching function presented in Chapter 6, we obtain $q(\theta) = M / V = a\theta^{-\eta}$.

The zero-profit condition implies that

$$J = \frac{pc}{a\theta^{-\eta}}. \tag{7.2}$$

Further, the present discounted value of the expected profit from an occupied job, J, is given by

$$rJ = p - w - \lambda J, \tag{7.3}$$

where w represents wage and rJ is the capital cost of the job.

The job yields a net return of $p - w$ and also runs a destruction risk of λ. Note that in our model, J, w and P denote their average values of all the jobs in the region, because the firm does not know which worker will be matched in the future. Equations (7.2) and (7.3) thus imply the job creation condition below:

$$p - w - \frac{(r + \lambda)pc}{a\theta^{-\eta}} = 0. \tag{7.4}$$

Equation 7.4 is a determination condition for θ, which is the number of jobs created per unit of jobseekers, defined as $\theta \equiv V/(U + \phi S^e + \varphi S^m)$. This equation indicates that θ lowers if a decreases, because the present discounted value of the expected profit from a job vacancy decreases when matching efficiency declines; therefore, firms post fewer job vacancies when matching efficiency is lower. Further, we also expect higher productivity to create more jobs because it increases the profit of a filled position.[1]

Moreover, because Equation 7.4 is the determination equation of θ, θ will not change unless the factors of $(r + \lambda), p, c$ and w change. Since θ is defined as $\theta \equiv V/(U + \phi S^e + \varphi S^m)$, we obtain the determination equation of job vacancies as

$$V = \theta[p, w, (r + \lambda), c] * (U + \phi S^e + \varphi S^m). \tag{7.5}$$

As a result, under the condition of optimal firm behavior, more jobseekers leads to more job vacancies, but the higher number of jobseekers does not influence the job creation index, θ. This optimal behavior mainly refers to the adjustment of vacancies by firms, by which θ satisfies Equation (7.4) even when the number of jobseekers changes, by creating or removing vacancies.

7.2.2 Wage Determination

The job creation condition shown in Equation (7.4) also includes an endogenous variable of wage, which is determined by the behaviors of workers and firms as well as by the market environment. When a job is matched, the worker gives up unemployment returns, U', and gains returns from being employed, W. At the same time, the firm gives up its returns from the vacant job, V', and receives returns from the profit of the occupied job, J. The net returns of the worker and firm from the match, $W - U'$ and $J - V'$ respectively, are therefore determined by the generalized Nash

---

1.   This is easier to understand by substituting $p - w - \dfrac{(r + \lambda)pc}{a\theta^{-\eta}} = 0$ into $1 - \dfrac{w}{p} - \dfrac{(r + \lambda)c}{a\theta^{-\eta}} = 0$.

bargaining problem. Note that the average wage considered in this chapter, treated as a determinant of job creation, is that of total workers (i.e., including both residents and migrants).

First, the present discounted value of the expected income stream of an employed worker, W, is obtained from the following Bellman equation:

$$rW = w + \lambda(U'-W), \tag{7.6}$$

where w is the average wage and U' is the present discounted value of the expected income stream of an unemployed worker.

In this equation, rW, the capital cost of the asset of the occupied job, equals wage, w, to which the risk of being unemployed, $\lambda(U'-W)$, is added.

Further, the rate at which a jobseeker becomes employed is $\theta q(\theta)$.[2] We assume that unemployment benefit is zero in this model because China's unemployment insurance and subsidy system had not been fully implemented during our sample period.[3] Therefore, the present discounted value of the expected income stream of an unemployed worker, U', satisfies the following Bellman equation:

$$rU' = \theta q(\theta)(W - U'), \tag{7.7}$$

where the capital cost of the asset of the state of unemployment compensates for the probability that the unemployed worker matches a job, $\theta q(\theta)(W - U')$.

Finally, the wage satisfies the Nash bargaining solution,

$$w = \arg\max(W - U')^{\beta}(J - V')^{1-\beta}, \tag{7.8}$$

where β measures labor bargaining power.

The first-order condition is solved as

$$W - U' = \beta(J + W - V - U'). \tag{7.9}$$

---

2. The rate at which a jobseeker gains employment is denoted by $M/(U + \phi S^e + \varphi S^m)$. Since $q(\theta) = M/V$ and $M = a(U + \phi S^e + \varphi S^m)^{\eta} V^{1-\eta}$, the rate at which a jobseeker gains employment is $M/(U + \phi S^e + \varphi S^m) = \theta q(\theta)$.

3. Because unemployment insurance only exists in certain regions and for certain workers, the estimation combines the possible effects of unemployment insurance in certain regions in the unobserved term of c_i^w.

From Equations (7.3), (7.6) and (7.9), and also the equilibrium condition $V = 0$, we derive the following relationship:

$$w = rU' + \beta(p - rU'). \tag{7.10}$$

Then, Equations (7.2), (7.7), (7.9) and (7.10) lead to the following condition:

$$rU' = \frac{\beta}{1-\beta} \, pc\theta. \tag{7.11}$$

By substituting (7.11) into (7.10), we finally obtain the wage determination equation:

$$w = \beta p(1 + c\theta). \tag{7.12}$$

7.3   Estimation and Results

Data on jobseekers and job creation come from the labor agencies in China, which provide annual figures for the number of job vacancies (NBS 1997–2009a). The job creation index, θ, is calculated by $\theta \equiv V /(U + \phi S^e + \varphi S^m)$, where ϕ and φ are based on the estimated results derived from Model (4) originally presented in Chapter 6. Note that unemployed jobseekers include both registered unemployed workers and laid-off workers. Data on the matching efficiencies of the total market are also obtained from Model (4). Other data, such as productivity, average wages, employment and job destruction, come from NBS (1997–2009b), taken directly or with several adjustments as before. Data on productivity and average wages are real figures, after price index adjustments. The period covered is 1996–2008, and the analysis comprises a cross-section of the 29 Chinese provinces investigated.[4] Data description and summary statistics for the job creation model are reported in Table 7.1.

---

4. Recall that Hong Kong, Macau, Xinjiang, Tibet and Taiwan are excluded.

Table 7.1 Data description and summary statistics for the job creation model

Var.	Definition	Data description	Mean	Std. Dev.	Obs.
U_{it}	Unemployed job seekers	Number of unemployed job seekers in job agencies (10,000 persons)	43.40	51.01	372
S_{it}^e	Employed job seekers	Number of employed job seekers in job agencies (10,000 persons)	18.67	33.91	186
S_{it}^m	Migrant job seekers	Number of migrant job seekers in job agencies (10,000 persons)	49.17	75.16	197
V_{it}	Job vacancies	Number of vacant jobs in job agencies (10,000 persons)	96.99	154.02	376
w_{it}	Wage	Average wage of urban employed workers (*yuan*)	11594.75	5946.78	346
λ_{it}	Job destruction rate	The ratio of annual inflows into registered unemployment and layoff to total employment	0.06	0.04	174
θ_{it}	Market tightness	$\theta = V /(U + \phi S^e + \varphi S^m)$	0.47	0.14	187
P_{it}	Productivity	Annual average production per worker (labor productivity; *yuan*)	33966.34	19280.83	375
r_{it}	Interest rate	Average real lending rate for the year	0.08	0.06	172

Sources: NBS 1997–2009a, NBS 1997–2009b.

For the estimation of Equations (7.4) and (7.12), we estimate c and β as coefficients and let $c = \beta^c, \beta = \beta^\beta$. Since β exists in both Equations (7.4) and (7.12), our estimation includes the constraints between the two equations. The estimation equations are as follows:

$$p_{it} - w_{it} = \beta^c \frac{(r_{it} + \lambda_{it})p_{it}}{a\theta_{it}^{-\eta}} + c_i^\theta + \varepsilon_{it}^\theta, \tag{7.13}$$

$$w_{it} = \beta^\beta p_{it} + \beta^\beta \beta^c p_{it}\theta_{it} + c^w + c_i^w + \varepsilon_{it}^w, \tag{7.14}$$

where i denotes the 29 provinces, t denotes the years, β^c and β^β represent the estimated coefficients, ε_{it}^x s stand for residuals, and c_i^x denotes the fixed effects of regions.

Because of the possible correlation between the independent variables and residuals, we introduce instruments for Equation (7.14). The variables being instrumented are p_{it} and $p_{it}\theta_{it}$, and we choose $p_{i,t-1}$ and $p_{i,t-1}\theta_{i,t-1}$ as instruments for them. The relevance and exogeneity of these instruments are also examined. We use the 3SLS approach for the estimation of the two-equation system of Equations (7.13) and (7.14) (see Table 7.2). For comparison purposes, we also list the results of other methods, such as the OLS, 2SLS, Full Information Maximum Likelihood (FIML), GMM, and SUR procedures.

Based on these estimation results, we obtain the following econometric model of urban job creation in China. Note that in Equation (7.15), we have transferred the original structural form into the determination equation of θ, and substituted η with 0.8, which was obtained in Chapter 6 as an estimate of η:

$$\theta_{it} = [\frac{1}{a_{it}}[0.76 \frac{(r_{it} + \lambda_{it})p_{it}}{(p_{it} - w_{it} - 11806.75 - c_i^\theta - \varepsilon_{it}^\theta)}]]^{-\frac{1}{0.8}}, \qquad (7.15)$$

$$(5.0)*** \qquad\qquad (3.4)*** \qquad\qquad (5.4)***$$

$$(\text{Adj. } R = 0.82)$$

$$w_{it} = 0.26 p_{it} + 0.26 * 0.76 p_{it}\theta_{it} + 5175.97 + c_i^w + \varepsilon_{it}^w, \qquad (7.16)$$

$$(12.7)*** \ (12.7)*** \ (5.0)*** \quad (5.1)*** \qquad (\text{Adj. } R = 0.99)$$

$$V_{it} = \theta_{it}(U_{it} + 2.06 S_{it}^e + 2.06 S_{it}^m). \qquad (7.17)$$

In the presented model, the number of job vacancies is determined by Equation (7.17), given the prospect of optimal job creation. As discussed in Section 5.1, if firms' job creation behavior is optimal, market tightness, θ, which is defined by $\theta \equiv V/(U + \phi S^e + \varphi S^m)$, cannot be affected by changes in the number of jobseekers, because if the number of jobseekers increases, posting job vacancies would become profitable, firms would create more jobs, and the ratio of V to $(U + \phi S^e + \varphi S^m)$ would thus not change. To confirm this point, we regressed the residual of Equation (7.15) on S^e and S^m and found rather insignificant coefficients. Further, the Wald test does not reject the null hypothesis that the coefficients of S^e and S^m are zero, indicating that S^e and S^m do not change market tightness. This result is consistent with the findings of the structural estimation in Chapter 4, as well as the results derived from the reduced-form estimations presented by Knight et al. (1999), Knight and Yueh (2004), and Meng and Zhang (2010). These studies used different methods in order to show that an increase of migrants in urban areas does not lead to greater urban unemployment.

Table 7.2 Estimation results of the job creation determination model

Dep. Var.: $(p_{it} - w_{it})$	Model	Comparison			
Var.	3SLS	OLS	2SLS	W2SLS	SUR
$(r_{it} + \lambda_{it})p_{it}$ $q(\theta_{it})$	0.76	0.10	0.76	0.76	0.006
	[4.98]***	[2.22]**	[5.86]***	[4.98]***	[0.19]
Const.	11806.75	13681.03	18672.19	18672.18	19972.91
	[3.38]***	[6.54]***	[3.97]***	[3.38]***	[3.41]***
R	0.91	0.90	0.91	0.91	0.89
Adj. R	0.87	0.85	0.87	0.87	0.84
N	104	104	104	104	104

Dep. Var.: w_{it}	Model	Comparison			
Var.	3SLS	OLS	2SLS	W2SLS	SUR
p_{it} or β^{β} [a]	0.26	0.35	0.26	0.26	0.38
	[12.69]***	[20.04]***	[13.50]***	[12.86]***	[30.20]***
$p_{it}\theta_{it}$ or β^{c} [b]	0.76	0.10	0.76	0.76	0.006
	[4.98]***	[2.22]**	[5.86]***	[4.98]***	[0.19]
Const.	5175.97	4472.96	5176.02	5176.03	4121.12
	[5.05]***	[4.38]***	[4.23]***	[5.05]***	[5.80]***
R	0.71	0.84	0.71	0.71	0.85
Adj. R	0.68	0.83	0.68	0.68	0.83
N	339	368	339	339	368

a These are the coefficients of p_{it} in the OLS, 2SLS, FIML and GMM methods, and the estimate of β^{β} in the cases of 3SLS and SUR.
b These are the coefficients of $p_{it}\theta_{it}$ in the OLS, 2SLS, FIML and GMM methods, and the estimate of β^{c} in the cases of 3SLS and SUR.

Note: *p < 0.1, **p < 0.05, ***p < 0.01

7.4   Discussion

In the estimation results of job creation, the coefficient is significant and consistent with search theory, implying that the presented job creation model is appropriate for use to explain job creation in China. Firms project their expected profits from vacant and occupied jobs, and decide how many jobs to create in order to maximize their profits. For confirmation of this finding, we ran a reduced-form estimation and found similar results (details are reported in Appendix 7.A).

Therefore, we have shown that in China, matching efficiency, a, and productivity, P, positively affect job creation, whereas the interest rate, r, and job destruction rate, λ, negatively influence job creation. First, matching efficiency increases job creation because when a firm opens up a vacancy, there is a risk that the vacant job might not be matched to a worker (and therefore only results in advertisement expenses and time costs); a higher matching efficiency in China's labor market could thereby reduce that risk. This result reveals one of the reasons why regions that have more efficient labor exchanges, such as Shanghai and Guangzhou, house firms that create a greater number of job opportunities.

Second, productivity plays an important role in job creation. As a developing country, China's productivity is growing rapidly. The higher its level of productivity, the more profitable creating new jobs will be. This capitalization effect of productivity growth is considerable in China.

Third, a lower interest rate, r, can also increase job creation in China. A decrease in lending rates would lead to lower capital costs for firms and encourage them to expand their production scales and thereby create more jobs. The policy of changing interest rates has been adopted frequently in China (15 times during 2002–2008),[5] and the effect of this on the production of firms cannot be ignored.

Finally, our results show that the rate of job destruction, λ, negatively affects job creation in China, as the expected returns from an occupied job decrease when there is high job destruction, and consequently firms create fewer jobs. This finding explains the generally opposite trends of job creation and job destruction in China, as described in Chapter 5.

---

5. "*Li lv li ci tiao zheng yi lang*" (A list of interest rate adjustments, by the Central Bank of China). http://data.eastmoney.com/cjsj/yhll.html.

As an aside, we also find that wages increase with productivity growth and that market tightness positively influences wages. However, although the adjusted R-squared values for these factors are high, average urban wages are not completely determined by productivity and market tightness, because there are large constant and fixed-effect terms that denote unobserved variables. The most likely reason for this result is that a considerable proportion of the wages of urban residents is not completely determined by the profit maximization behavior of firms, but rather by institutional factors, such as the remaining influence of the planned economy. Nevertheless, the model captures the effects of productivity and market tightness on wage levels, thereby enabling the analysis of endogenous job creation in China.

7.5 Conclusions

China has made great strides towards a market economy over the past two decades. In this chapter, we found that job creation in the 1990s and 2000s in China was determined significantly by productivity, market efficiency, interest rates and job destruction, which are factors that characterize the optimizing behaviors of firms and workers based on search and matching theory. Further, job creation in China reacts efficiently to changes in jobseekers, because an increase in the number of jobseekers does not change the ratio of vacant jobs to jobseekers.

Further, the rate of job creation increases with productivity growth, because firms create more jobs when larger profits are available, and higher productivity leads to larger profits. As a developing country, China's technological catch-up and management improvements in enterprises, such as the reform of SOEs and development of private firms, are leading to rapidly growing productivity, which contributes significantly to job creation.

However, a decline in job–worker matching efficiency, as found in Chapter 6, negatively influences job creation, because it increases the possibility of a vacant job not being matched to a worker as matching efficiency decreases, which discourages firms from creating jobs. In summary, declining matching efficiency affects China's labor market in two distinct ways: it reduces new hires (given a certain number of vacancies and jobseekers, as observed in Chapter 6) and negatively influences job creation.

Further, the increased job destruction in the 1990s restrained job creation in China, because firms tend to create fewer jobs if there is a higher possibility of them being destroyed. As shown in Figs. 5.3 and 5.4, job creation dropped greatly in the late 1990s when job destruction peaked both in state-owned and in private enterprises.

Based on the foregoing, it is important that job creation reacts effectively to changes in the number of jobseekers. The theoretical job creation condition indicates that under profit maximization, θ, the ratio of vacant jobs to jobseekers, is independent of changes in the number of jobseekers, which is the reality in China, as described in this chapter. This finding is especially important for examining how rural–urban migrants affect China's labor market. Although more migrant jobseekers are moving to cities in China, they have not changed the market tightness because firms have opened up more vacancies as the number of jobseekers are increasing.

These processes that determine the levels of job creation and wages indicate that the labor market in China performed better over the past two decades. However, as in most developed and developing countries, frictions in the labor market are considerable. In Chapter 8 we will make use of the findings of the matching function and job creation determination in a labor market model in order to examine the determinants of urban unemployment under the search and matching approach.

Appendix 7A Confirmation from the reduced-form estimations

For confirmation of the result obtained by our structural estimation, we ran the linear reduced-form estimation, and the results are reported in Table 7.3.

The result indicates that productivity and matching efficiency have a significant positive coefficient and that the interest rate has a significant negative coefficient for job creation in China, which is consistent with that found by using the structural model. Note that this is not the real econometric model of job creation in China, because the actual relations between factors are not a simple linear form of this reduced estimation, and the cautions are unclear. We only ran this estimation for a robustness check of our structural estimation result.

Table 7.3 Results of the reduced-form estimation

(1) Dependent Variable: V (Number of vacant jobs)

	Model 1	Model 2	Model 3	Model 4	Model 5
	OLS	OLS	OLS	OLS	2SLS
$\ln p_{it}$	1.19	0.57	0.21	0.27	0.24
	[9.27]***	[7.81]***	[3.40]***	[4.28]***	[3.56]***
$\ln a_{it}$	−0.03	0.62	0.42	0.14	0.40
	[−0.12]	[5.12]***	[4.40]***	[1.20]	[2.75]***
$\ln r_{it}$	−0.15	−0.14	−0.09	−0.09	−0.10
	[−2.08]**	[−3.55]***	[−2.96]***	[−3.19]***	[−3.19]***
$\ln \lambda_{it}$	0.09	0.05	0.04	0.05	0.04
	[1.29]	[1.36]	[1.35]	[1.65]*	[1.33]
$\ln(S_{it}^e + S_{it}^m)$		0.76	0.58	0.53	0.65
		[26.59]***	[22.61]***	[18.18]***	[14.50]***
$\ln U_{it}$			0.41	0.34	0.32
			[13.49]***	[9.98]***	[8.81]***
$\ln je_{it}$				0.15	0.07
				[3.91]***	[1.40]
Const.	−8.49	−4.80	−1.76	−2.94	−2.49
	[−6.02]***	[−6.21]***	[−2.73]***	[−4.21]***	[−3.24]***
R.	0.36	0.82	0.89	0.89	0.89
Adj. R.	0.36	0.82	0.89	0.89	0.89
N.	293	292	292	292	291

Instruments for 2SLS: $\ln p_{i,t-1}$ $\ln je_{i,t-1}$ $\ln(S_{i,t-1}^e + S_{i,t-1}^m)$

(2) Dependent Variable: V/S (Number of vacant jobs/Number of job seekers)

	Model 6	Model 7	Model 8	Model 9	Model 10
	OLS	OLS	OLS	OLS	2SLS
$\ln p_{it}$	0.21	0.23	0.14	0.20	0.17
	[3.98]***	[4.06]***	[2.23]**	[3.17]***	[2.63]***
$\ln a_{it}$	0.49	0.48	0.42	0.13	0.36
	[5.32]***	[5.01]***	[4.50]***	[1.14]	[2.61]***
$\ln r_{it}$	−0.10	−0.10	−0.09	−0.10	−0.10
	[−3.42]***	[−3.48]***	[−3.11]***	[−3.36]***	[−3.42]***
$\ln \lambda_{it}$	0.04	0.04	0.04	0.05	0.04
	[1.32]	[1.39]	[1.32]	[1.64]	[1.36]
$\ln(S_{it}^{e} + S_{it}^{m})$		−0.03	−0.07	−0.13	−0.02
		[−1.23]	[−2.93]***	[−4.67]***	[−0.57]
$\ln U_{it}$			0.11	0.04	0.02
			[3.68]***	[1.18]	[0.61]
$\ln je_{it}$				0.16	0.09
				[4.14]***	[1.76]*
Const.	−3.04	−3.13	−2.32	−3.53	−3.14
	[−5.14]***	[−5.19]***	[−3.69]***	[−5.21]***	[−4.28]***
R.	0.14	0.15	0.19	0.23	0.19
Adj. R.	0.13	0.13	0.17	0.21	0.17
N.	293	292	292	292	291
Instruments for 2SLS:		$\ln p_{i,t-1}$	$\ln je_{i,t-1}$	$\ln(S_{i,t-1}^{e} + S_{i,t-1}^{m})$	

Note: *p < 0.1, **p < 0.05, ***p < 0.01

8

Unemployment Evolution and the Beveridge Curve

8.1 Introduction

High job and worker reallocations, declining labor market matching efficiency, and active job creation enlighten a novel approach for us to tackle the unemployment problem in China. Numerous studies have examined labor market matching and unemployment in developed countries using search and matching models, which effectively take into account the imperfect information and frictions prevalent in the labor market. However, such frictions in the labor market persist not only in developed countries but also in developing economies, because economic transitions and technology advancements often lead to high job rotation and worker reallocation, even though quantitative studies of search and matching in the labor markets of developing countries, especially China, are scarce. Based on the analysis presented in Chapters 5–7, this chapter constructs an econometric model and uses a search and matching approach in order to tackle the issue of high unemployment in China.

Unlike those studies that have examined the determinants of unemployed individuals, such as education and gender (Liu, Q. 2012; Knight and Song 2005; Xie 2008), we pay attention to macro-level movements in the unemployment rate by examining the principal issues of aggregate labor market matching, as well as job creation and destruction, in a multi-model unemployment framework. In particular, we shed light on the unemployment mechanism in order to capture the relationships among different factors by examining the various channels that lead to unemployment. For instance, productivity growth can worsen unemployment by accelerating job destruction, but can also contribute to employment by encouraging the creation of new jobs.

As discussed in previous chapters, despite the rapid economic growth in China and the large number of job opportunities created across the country, the unemployment rate remains rather high. For instance, in 2006, the unemployment rate in Fujian province, including laid-off workers, was approximately 7%,[1] while a survey reported that 86% of firms in the southeast of Fujian province found it difficult to recruit enough workers (Cai et al. 2007). However, the notion that unemployment is caused by a gap between labor supply and demand has been unable to explain the simultaneous coexistence of high unemployment and high job vacancies (Rogerson et al. 2005). This coexistence actually occurs because of the economic reality of imperfect information; jobseekers and job vacancies are no longer assumed to match immediately but rather proceed through a search and matching process in which some workers may not find work, while some firms have positions that remain vacant.

Search and matching theory successfully integrates imperfect information into labor market modeling. Such an employment process matches jobseekers to job vacancies based on a matching efficiency scale (Diamond and Maskin 1979; Blanchard and Diamond 1994; Pissarides 2000). Starting from this notion of a matching function, Pissarides (2000) constructed a series of conditions that jointly determine labor market outcomes, namely job creation (with endogenous wage determination), job destruction, and on-the-job searches.[2] These conditions define the process of job-worker matching, the level of job creation, the level of endogenous job destruction, and the amount of on-the-job searches in order to indicate overall unemployment evolution. Using this theoretical framework, in this chapter, we construct an empirical search and matching model for China's labor market.

In the latter part of this chapter, we will examine China's Beveridge curve (BC), which describes the relationship between equilibrium unemployment and job vacancies in the country, and which has been widely used to examine issues of labor economics. A shift in the BC reflects both structural changes and economic shocks (Cahuc and Zylberberg 2004), as observed in many countries (Samson 1994; Wall and Zoega 2002). Our model derives the Beveridge function of China in order to highlight how

---

1. According to NBS (2007a), the official unemployment rate in Fujian province was 3.9% and the number of unemployed workers was 151,000. However, since 129,000 laid-off workers in Fujian province were excluded from this figure, the real unemployment rate could be as high as 7%.
2. This case considers on-the-job searches in Pissarides (2000).

structural changes and economic shocks have shifted the BC and JC. The result is consistent with the country's historical unemployment-vacancy (U-V) curve.

The remainder of this chapter is organized as follows. Section 8.2 describes the data used in this study. Section 8.3 constructs the econometric model of unemployment evolution in China, which is used to examine the effects of matching efficiency, job destruction, job-search services and productivity, using a series of simulations in Section 8.4. Section 8.5 discusses the determinants of the BC shifts in China. Section 8.6 concludes.

8.2   Data

We sourced the presented data on job vacancies, jobseekers and new hires from approximately 30,000 public and private labor agencies in China (NBS 1997–2009a), as explained in Chapter 6. Again, the period covered was 1996–2008, the analysis covered a cross-section of 29 Chinese provinces[3]. Similarly, we used the number of job agencies per employment scale, je, as the index of job-search services. All other macro data were derived and adjusted as described before. The data and summary statistics are described in Table 8.1.

8.3   Econometric Model of Unemployment Evolution in China

Our structural model of China's unemployment is based on Pissarides 2000,[4] which models the macro-level labor market using the search and matching approach in order to determine unemployment evolution. We apply this model to China by introducing the heterogeneity between jobseeker groups and rural–urban migration. Hence, our structural model consists of job–worker matching with heterogeneous jobseekers, job creation, job destruction, the job searches of migrants and employed workers, and unemployment evolution. See Table 8.1 for the details of the endogenous and exogenous variables used in the presented model.

---

3. As before, Hong Kong, Macau, Xinjiang, Tibet and Taiwan are excluded.
4. Pissarides 2000, chap. 1 and chap. 4.

Table 8.1 Data descriptions and summary statistics
for the unemployment model

Var.	Definition	Data description	Mean	Std. Dev.	Obs.
Endogenous variables					
S_{it}	Jobseekers	Number of jobseekers in job agencies (10,000 persons)	100.00	121.28	376
M_{it}	New hires	Number of average annual new hires in job agencies (10,000 persons)	53.32	57.54	376
U_{it}	Unemployed jobseekers	Number of unemployed jobseekers in job agencies (10,000 persons)	43.40	51.01	372
S_{it}^{e}	Employed jobseekers	Number of employed jobseekers in job agencies (10,000 persons)	18.67	33.91	186
S_{it}^{m}	Migrant jobseekers	Number of migrant jobseekers in job agencies (10,000 persons)	49.17	75.16	197
V_{it}	Job vacancies	Number of vacant jobs in job agencies (10,000 persons)	96.99	154.02	376
H_{it}^{u}	New hires from unemployed jobseekers	Number of average annual new hires from unemployed workers in job agencies (10,000 persons)	23.15	23.76	368
H_{it}^{e}	New hires from employed jobseekers	Number of average annual new hires from employed jobseekers in job agencies (10,000 persons)	8.99	14.93	189
H_{it}^{m}	New hires from migrant jobseekers	Number of average annual new hires from migrant jobseekers in job agencies (10,000 persons)	29.28	35.10	195
w_{it}	Wage	Average wage of urban employed workers (*yuan*)	11594.75	5946.78	346

Table 8.1 (continued)

Exogenous variables

Var.	Definition	Data description	Mean	Std. Dev.	Obs.
λ_{it}	Job destruction rate	The ratio of annual inflows into registered unemployment and layoff to total employment	0.06	0.04	174
θ_{it}	Market tightness	$\theta = V/(U + \phi S^e + \varphi S^m)$	0.47	0.14	187
JE_{it}	Job search service	Number of job agencies	1115.31	716.51	375
P_{it}	Productivity	Annual average production per worker (labor productivity; *yuan*)	33966.34	19280.83	375
r_{it}	Interest rate	Average real lending rate for the year	0.08	0.06	172
E_{it}	General employment scale	Number of employed workers in the secondary and tertiary industries (10,000 persons)	1141.65	772.54	346
L_{it}^{RE}	Labor force of urban residents	Total number of employed and unemployed urban residents (10,000 persons)	340.53	181.89	319
B_{it}	Births	Annual number of new entrants into unemployment other than those through job destruction (10,000 persons)	16.53	12.11	201
D_{it}	Deaths	Annual number of new exits out of unemployment other than those through employment (10,000 persons)	2.04	3.84	200

Sources: NBS 1997–2009a, NBS 1997–2009b.

8.3.1 Theoretical model

Labor market matching

The models of labor market matching and job creation were described in Chapters 6 and 7. In summary, the matching function of China's labor market is assumed to be the following equation:

$$M = a(U + \phi S^e + \varphi S^m)^\eta V^{1-\eta}, \tag{8.1.1}$$

where M represents total new hires, U is the number of unemployed jobseekers, S^e is the number of employed urban jobseekers, and S^m is the number of migrant jobseekers. Further, V represents total notified job vacancies, ϕ and φ denote the heterogeneities of the three labor groups in the matching process, η and $\eta - 1$ measure the elasticity of jobseekers and job vacancies with respect to new hires, respectively, and a represents matching efficiency, which varies by year and region.

Further, the number of new hires from unemployment, H^u, is determined by

$$H^u = a^u U^{\eta_1^u} V^{\eta_2^u} e^{\delta^{ue}(S^e/S)} e^{\delta^{um}(S^m/S)}, \tag{8.1.2}$$

where S is the total number of jobseekers, and S^e/S and S^m/S are the indices of congestion externalities from the other groups of jobseekers, with the coefficients of δ^{ue} and δ^{um} respectively.

The matching efficiency of the whole labor market, a, is an important factor for firms' job creation behavior, while the matching efficiency of unemployed workers, a^u, directly determines outflow from unemployment. These two matching efficiencies, a and a^u, are determined as follows:

$$a = a^{en}(je, \Delta p, \lambda) + a^{ex}, \tag{8.1.3}$$

$$a^u = a_u^{en}(je, \Delta p, \lambda) + a_u^{ex}, \tag{8.1.4}$$

where the endogenous parts, a^{en} and a_u^{en}, are determined by the job-search services provided by job agencies, je, productivity changes, Δp, and the job destruction rate, λ. a_u^{ex} and a^{ex} are the exogenous parts, which could be influenced by labor-market frictions.

Job creation

As discussed in Chapter 7, the job creation index, θ, which is defined as $\theta \equiv V / (U + \phi S^e + \varphi S^m)$, is determined by the following condition:

$$p - w - \frac{(r + \lambda)pc}{a\theta^{-\eta}} = 0, \tag{8.2.1}$$

where r denotes the interest rate, w denotes wage, p is the value of a job's output, pc is the cost of a vacant job for firms engaging in hiring, and $a\theta^{-\eta}$ is the probability of filling a vacant job per unit of time in the labor market, which is obtained from $q(\theta) = M / V = a\theta^{-\eta}$.

Furthermore, we obtain the determination equation of job vacancies as

$$V = \theta[p, w, (r + \lambda), c] \times (U + \phi S^e + \varphi S^m), \tag{8.2.2}$$

where $\theta[p, w, (r + \lambda), c]$ denotes that θ is a function of $p, w, (r + \lambda)$ and c, as indicated by Equation (8.2.1).

Further, the job creation condition equation (8.2.1) includes an endogenous variable of wage, which is given as follows:

$$w = \beta p(1 + c\theta), \tag{8.2.3}$$

where β measures labor bargaining power.

Job destruction

Job destruction refers to when firms dismiss workers and cause involuntary unemployment; this excludes job-to-job transfers. Job destruction can thus be divided into endogenous and exogenous parts. Endogenous job destruction is often caused by productivity growth, because higher productivity can destroy a greater number of jobs. For example, during China's economic development, regions that have higher productivity have shown rapid technology progress, while jobs that previously used old equipment have become profitless, leading to creative destruction (Cahuc and Zylberberg 2004). Moreover, a higher level of technology often leads to labor savings, which make it possible to obtain the same level of output with fewer workers. We also control the effect of market tightness, θ, which may influence endogenous job destruction (Pissarides 2000, 43–44).

Accordingly, we assume the job destruction equation to be as follows:

$$\lambda = \lambda^{en}(p,\theta) + \lambda^{ex},\tag{8.3}$$

where λ^{ex} represents the exogenous shocks of λ, and λ^{en} represents the endogenous component of λ.

Determinants of employed jobseekers

Our determination of employed jobseekers, S^e, is generally based on the reduced-form estimation presented by Pissarides (2000, chap. 4). The number of workers who conduct on-the-job searches for alternative jobs is determined by market tightness, θ, productivity level, P, and job-search services, je (which are all direct theoretical factors) as well as the job destruction rate, λ, an important factor in China because of the shocks caused by enterprise reform. We also control the effect of employment scale, E. The determination equation of S^e is provided as follows:

$$S^e = S^e(\lambda, p, je, \theta, E).\tag{8.4}$$

Determinant of migrant jobseekers

Given the large-scale rural–urban migration in the sample period, the most important determinant could be the higher wages in urban areas compared with those in rural regions. This could also be influenced by the same factors that determine the number of employed jobseekers, S^e, such as market tightness, θ, productivity level, P, job-search services, je, and job destruction rate, λ. Therefore, the determination equation of S^m is as follows:

$$S^m = S^m(w, \lambda, p, \theta, je).\tag{8.5}$$

Mean unemployment evolution

Mean unemployment evolution can be given by

$$\dot{U} = B + \lambda(L^{RE} - U) - H^U - D,\tag{8.6}$$

where $\dot{U}$ denotes mean unemployment evolution, which is defined as changes in the number of unemployed resident workers, λ is the job destruction rate, L^{RE} is the urban resident labor force, B is the number of new entrants into unemployment other than those due to job destruction (such as new graduates), and D is the number of new exits from unemployment other than those due to matching to a new job (such as retirements, layoffs and deaths). H^U represents the number of new hires from unemployed workers, which is determined by equation (8.1.2).

8.3.2 Estimation and results

In the presented theoretical model, there are seven endogenous variables and seven unique determination equations. We use 3SLS analysis for the estimation and introduce instruments for the endogenous variables, which also appear as explanatory variables in this model. Table 8.2 shows the estimation equations, together with the instrumented variables. The equations without an instrument listed do not include the instrumented variables. We also use instruments for p in the job creation and job destruction equations, because our productivity data are those of labor productivity endogenously correlated with the number of workers. The relevance and exogeneity of the instruments are also examined.

For the estimation of the condition for job creation (e.8.2.1) and wage determination (e.8.2.3), we estimate c and β as coefficients. Since β exists in both Equations (e.8.2.1) and (e.8.2.3), our estimation includes the constraints between them.

The details of the estimation results are reported in Appendix 8A (Table 8.6), while the econometric model of urban unemployment is shown in Table 8.3. Note that the matching functions in the econometric model are those obtained in Chapter 6. For the matching function of the entire labor market, considering the possible correlation between the independent variables and disturbance, we choose Model (4), which includes the instrumental variables and covers the entire period of study from 1996 to 2008. The matching function of unemployed workers is that obtained from the separate matching functions of the three jobseeker groups in Chapter 6.

Table 8.2 Estimation system of the unemployment evolution model

	Estimation equation	No.
Job–worker matching	$a_{it} = \beta^{aj} je_{it} + \beta^{ap} \Delta p_{it} + \beta^{a\lambda} \lambda_{it} + c^a + c_i + a^{ex}$	(e.8.1.3)
	$a_{it}^u = \beta^{auj} je_{it} + \beta^{aup} \Delta p_{it} + \beta^{au\lambda} \lambda_{it} + c^{au} + c_i^u + a_u^{ex}$	(e.8.1.4)
Job creation	$p_{it} - w_{it} = c \dfrac{(r_{it} + \lambda_{it}) p_{it}}{a_{it} \theta_{it}^{-\eta}} + c_i^\theta + c_t^\theta + \varepsilon_{it}^\theta$	(e.8.2.1)
	$w_{it} = \beta p_{it} + (\beta c) p_{it} \theta_{it} + c^w + c_i^w + \varepsilon_{it}^w$ Instrumented variables: p_{it}, $p_{it}\theta_{it}$ Instruments: $p_{i,t-1}$, $p_{i,t-1}\theta_{i,t-1}$	(e.8.2.3)
Job destruction	$\lambda_{it} = \beta^{\lambda p} p_{it} + \beta^{\lambda \theta} \theta_{it} + c^\lambda + c_t^\lambda + \lambda^{ex}$ Instrumented variables: p_{it}, θ_{it} Instruments: $p_{i,t-1}$, $\theta_{i,t-1}$	(e.8.3)
Employed jobseekers	$\log S_{it}^e = \beta^{se\lambda} \log \lambda_{it} + \beta^{sep} \log p_{it} + \beta^{se\theta} \log \theta_{it}$ $+ \beta^{se\sigma} \log je_{it} + \beta^{seE} \log E_{it} + c^{se} + c_t^{se} + \varepsilon_{it}^{se}$ Instrumented variables: $\log \theta_{it}$ Instruments: $\log \theta_{i,t-1}$	(e.8.4)
Migrant jobseekers	$\log S_{it}^m = \beta^{sm\lambda} \log \lambda_{it} + \beta^{smp} \log p_{it} + \beta^{sm\theta} \log \theta_{it} +$ $\beta^{sm\sigma} \log je_{it} + \beta^{smw} \log w_{it} + c^{sm} + c_i^{sm} + \varepsilon_{it}^{sm}$ Instrumented variables: $\log \theta_{it}$, $\log \lambda_{it}$ Instruments: $\log \theta_{i,t-1}$, $\log \lambda_{i,t-1}$	(e.8.5)

Notes:
(1) c_i^x and c_t^x denote the fixed effects of regions and years, respectively.
(2) Equations (e8.2.1) and (e8.2.3) constitute the structural estimation form for the job creation condition. The estimated coefficients are c, hiring cost, and β, wage bargaining power. Note that Equation (e8.2.1) is not a determination equation for p or w.

Table 8.3 Estimation results of the unemployment evolution model in China

Job–worker matching	$\ln M_{it} = -0.93 + 0.81\ln(U_{it} + 2.06S_{it}^e + 2.06S_{it}^m) + (1 - 0.81)\ln V_{it}$ $\quad(-0.6)\quad(4.1)^{***}\qquad(0.5)\qquad(0.5)\qquad\quad(4.1)^{***}$ $+\, a_i + a_t + \varepsilon_{it}^m$ $\quad$ where $(a_i + a_t) \equiv \ln a_{it}$	(m.8.1.1) (Adj. R = 0.95)
	$\ln H_{it}^u = 0.53\ln U_{it} + 0.23\ln V_{it} + 0.51\dfrac{S_{it}^e}{S_{it}} + 0.13\dfrac{S_{it}^m}{S_{it}} + a_i^u + a_t^u + \varepsilon_{it}^u$ $\qquad(5.6)^{***}\qquad(2.1)^{**}\qquad(1.6)\qquad\quad(0.5)\qquad\quad$(Adj. R = 0.95) where $(a_i^u + a_t^u) \equiv \ln a_{it}^u$	(m.8.1.2)
	$a_{it} = 0.13\,je_{it} - 2.31\times10^{-5}\Delta p_{it} + 0.79\lambda_{it} + 0.77 + c_i + a^{ex}$ $\quad(5.2)^{***}\qquad(-5.1)\qquad\qquad(3.0)^{**}\quad(13.3)^{***}\quad$(Adj. R = 0.70)	(m.8.1.3)
	$a_{it}^u = 0.08\,je_{it} - 8.42\times10^{-5}\Delta p_{it} - 4.49\lambda_{it} + 1.00 + c_i^u + a_u^{ex}$ $\quad(1.3)\qquad\quad(-7.3)^{***}\qquad\quad(-6.6)^{***}\;(6.7)^{***}\quad$(Adj. R = 0.58)	(m.8.1.4)
Job creation	$\theta_{it} = [\dfrac{1}{a_{it}}[0.76\dfrac{(r_{it} + \lambda_{it})p_{it}}{(p_{it} - w_{it} - 11806.75 - c_i^\theta - \varepsilon_{it}^\theta)}]]^{-\frac{1}{0.8}}$ $\qquad\quad(5.0)^{***}\qquad\qquad(4.1)^{***}\qquad\qquad(4.1)^{***}\quad$(Adj. R = 0.82)	(m.8.2.1)
	$V_{it} = \theta_{it}(U_{it} + 2.06S_{it}^e + 2.06S_{it}^m)$	(m.8.2.2)
	$w_{it} = 0.26p_{it} + 0.26*0.76p_{it}\theta_{it} + 5175.97 + c_i^w + \varepsilon_{it}^w$ $\quad(12.7)^{***}\quad(12.7)^{***}\,(5.0)^{***}\qquad(5.1)^{***}\qquad\quad$(Adj. R = 0.68)	(m.8.2.3)
Job destruction	$\lambda_{it} = 6.93\times10^{-7}p_{it} + 0.07\theta_{it} - 0.01 + c_t^\lambda + \lambda^{ex}$ $\quad(5.0)^{***}\qquad\quad(1.6)\qquad(-0.6)\qquad\quad$(Adj. R = 0.07)	(m.8.3)
Employed jobseekers	$\log S_{it}^e = 0.24\log\lambda_{it} + 0.84\log p_{it} - 1.96\log\theta_{it}$ $\qquad\quad(1.4)\qquad\quad(3.7)^{***}\qquad(-1.5)$ $+\,0.06\log je_{it} + 0.98\log E_{it} - 13.48 + c_t^{se} + \varepsilon_{it}^{se}$ $\quad(0.44)\qquad\quad(6.3)^{***}\qquad(-4.9)\qquad\quad$(Adj. R = 0.59)	(m.8.4)
Migrant jobseekers	$\log S_{it}^m = -0.27\log\lambda_{it} - 0.07\log p_{it} + 2.12\log\theta_{it} + 0.62\log je_{it}$ $\qquad\quad(-0.6)\qquad\quad(-0.1)\qquad\quad(0.8)\qquad\quad(1.9)^*$ $+\,1.22\log w_{it} - 9.51 + c_i^{sm} + \varepsilon_{it}^{sm}$ $\quad(2.2)^{**}\qquad(-2.3)^{**}\qquad\qquad$(Adj. R = 0.63)	(m.8.5)
Growth in unemployment	$\dot{U} = B + \lambda(L^{RE} - U) - H^U - D$	(m.8.6)

Notes:

(1) In Equation (m.8.2.1), we transferred the original form into the determination equation of θ.

(2) Equations (m.8.2.2) and (m.8.6) are not estimated equations. Equation (m.8.2.2) is an identification based on the definition of job creation in Pissarides (2000), with estimation results of Equation (m.8.1.1) submitted. Equation (m.8.6) is the definition of unemployment evolution.

8.3.3 Discussion

The findings on labor market matching were discussed in detail in Chapter 6. We find that job-search services have significant positive effects on both matching efficiencies, while the job destruction rate, λ, has a significant positive effect on a but an insignificant negative effect on a^u, because most of the jobs destroyed in the enterprise reforms were in SOEs, which were more easily matched with unemployed residents than they were with other jobseekers.

For job creation, as examined in Chapter 7, matching efficiency, a, and productivity, P, have positive effects on job creation index, θ, while the job destruction rate, λ, has a negative effect on job creation. Further, firms create a larger number of jobs, V, if there are more jobseekers in the labor market. In the job destruction equation, Equation (8.3), the coefficient, P, is significantly positive, which is consistent with the theory of creative destruction following technological progress. However, the effect of market tightness on firms' job destruction decisions is not significant, perhaps because of China's underdeveloped labor market and high degree of imperfect information.

In the estimation results of employed Chinese jobseekers, productivity, P, has a significant positive effect on S^e, which is consistent with search theory (Pissarides 2000, 119–120). The higher productivity, the greater are the expected returns from job searches. For migrant jobseekers, w and je have significantly positive coefficients, indicating that higher wages or more job-search services could encourage greater rural–urban migration for jobs. Note that although market tightness, θ, also theoretically determines job searches according to Pissarides (2000), our estimates are insignificant for both employed jobseekers and migrant jobseekers. Therefore, in order to confirm this finding, we deleted θ from the determination equations of employment and migrant jobseekers, and found robust estimates of key factors and the entire equation (see Table 8.6.), indicating that the market environment has little effect on the job-search decisions of employed and migrant jobseekers.

Finally, we confirm that the above conditions, which involve job–worker matching, job creation, job destruction, and employed and migrant jobseekers, collectively determine unemployment evolution, $\dot{U} = B + \lambda(L^{RE} - U) - H^U - D$. As discussed above, the conditions comprise various factors, the most important of which should be matching efficiency shocks, job destruction shocks, productivity, and job-search services. Section 8.4 will explain how these factors affect unemployment through job–worker matching, endogenous job creation and destruction, and the job searches of non-unemployed jobseekers using simulations.

8.4   Simulations

Because the theoretical influences of job-search services and labor productivity are complicated and sometimes ambiguous, simulations provide an easy way to gauge their influences on China's labor market. Even without using simulations, we have already shown that a positive matching efficiency shock can decrease unemployment changes, and that a negative job destruction shock can lead to a high level of unemployment. However, since the extents of their effects on unemployment remain unclear, this subsection presents the results of the simulations run in order to clarify them.

8.4.1 Simulation results

Our simulations were carried out in the following manner. We first solved the model to obtain baseline solutions. Next, we ran four scenarios, in each of which we increased the value of all observations of a & a_u, λ, je and P by one standard deviation in order to solve the model again. Finally, we compared the scenarios and baseline solutions.

In the scenario of matching efficiency shocks, we treated a and a^u as the exogenous variables (deleting their determination) and increased them by one standard deviation (0.29 for a and 0.59 for a^u). Similarly, for the job destruction shocks, we treated λ as an exogenous variable (deleting its determination) and increased it by one standard deviation (0.04). In scenarios je and P, we considered all endogenous variables, including a, a^u and λ, and solved the model using their baseline and scenario data respectively. All the simulation results are reported in Tables 8.4 and 8.5.

Table 8.4 Simulation results of a^{ex} and λ^{ex}

	Scenario		Results						
1. Scenario of a^{ex}	a	a^u	dU	θ	w	S^m	S^e	λ	
Baseline	1.07	1.40	–2.45	1.39	29630.80	118.46	22.16	0.06	
(X^{Base})	(0.29)	(0.59)	(36.89)	(0.33)	(5742.62)	(127.78)	(20.81)	(0.03)	
Simulation 1	1.36	1.99	–19.89	1.50	30955.73	126.05	22.16	0.06	
(X^{Sim1})	(0.29)	(0.59)	(46.77)	(0.31)	(6417.44)	(141.09)	(20.81)	(0.03)	
$\dfrac{X^{Sim1}-X^{Base}}{\left|X^{Base}\right|}$	27.1%	42.1%	–711.8%	7.9%	4.5%	6.4%	0.0%	0.0%	

2. Scenario of λ^{ex}	λ	dU	θ	w	S^m	S^e	a	a^u
Baseline	0.05	–17.75	1.39	29758.38	133.11	20.75	1.05	1.43
(X^{Base})	(0.04)	(45.12)	(0.33)	(6058.57)	(156.18)	(19.65)	(0.23)	(0.47)
Simulation 2	0.09	0.77	1.40	29921.93	113.75	23.90	1.08	1.25
(X^{Sim2})	(0.04)	(42.08)	(0.33)	(6118.82)	(132.10)	(22.52)	(0.23)	(0.47)
$\dfrac{X^{Sim2}-X^{Base}}{\left|X^{Base}\right|}$	80.0%	104.3%	0.7%	0.5%	–14.5%	15.2%	2.9%	–12.6%

Table 8.5 Simulation results of je and P

	Scenario	Results							
3. Scenario of je	je	dU	θ	w	S^m	S^e	a_u	a	λ
Baseline	1.13	–12.59	1.39	29823.19	120.27	22.16	1.37	1.06	0.07
(X^{Base})	(0.68)	(47.38)	(0.33)	(6103.67)	(132.47)	(20.81)	(0.48)	(0.23)	(0.03)
Simulation 3	2.41	–14.05	1.45	30344.22	162.18	22.63	1.47	1.22	0.07
(X^{Sim3})	(1.94)	(47.55)	(0.32)	(6302.72)	(157.27)	(21.15)	(0.44)	(0.30)	(0.03)
$\dfrac{X^{Sim3}-X^{Base}}{\left|X^{Base}\right|}$	113.3%	–11.6%	4.3%	1.7%	34.8%	2.1%	7.3%	15.1%	0.0%

Table 8.5 (continued)

4. Scenario of $\dfrac{P}{P}$	P	dU	θ	w	S^m	S^e	a_u	a	λ
Baseline	53247.17	−12.59	1.39	29823.19	120.27	22.16	1.37	1.06	0.07
(X^{Base})	(19280.83)	(47.38)	(0.33)	(6103.67)	(132.47)	(20.81)	(0.48)	(0.23)	(0.03)
Simulation 4	72528.00	−8.08	1.73	45111.28	188.33	29.25	1.31	1.07	0.08
(X^{Sim4})	(19280.83)	(47.64)	(0.37)	(6374.99)	(186.49)	(26.69)	(0.48)	(0.23)	(0.03)
$\dfrac{X^{Sim4} - X^{Base}}{\left|X^{Base}\right|}$	36.2%	35.8%	24.5%	51.3%	56.6%	32.0%	−4.4%	0.9%	14.3%

Notes:
(1) All values denote the means of the observations, and their standard deviations are in parentheses.
(2) X stands for each variable in the columns, and $\left|X^{Base}\right|$ is the absolute value of the baseline solution of X. For instance, $(X^{Sim1} - X^{Base})/\left|X^{Base}\right|$ in the column of dU provides the increase in dU between its scenario and baseline solutions.
(3) The effects of market tightness, θ, on job destruction, employed jobseekers and migrant jobseekers are not considered because they have little effect on firms' and workers' decisions, as discussed in Section 8.4.

8.4.2 Discussion

Influences of matching efficiency shocks, a & a_u

The results here show that dU decreased greatly following an increase by one unit of standard deviation of a and a^u, for three reasons based on the simulation results shown in Table 8.4 and our econometric model. First, the growth in matching efficiency increases new hires, thereby directly decreasing unemployment (Equations (m.8.1.2) and (m.8.6)). Second, the job creation index, θ, is also increased by raising matching efficiency, a, by 7.9%, which has a further positive effect on decreasing unemployment (Equations (m.8.2.1), (m.8.2.2), (m.8.1.2) and (m.8.6)). Third, a higher θ leads to a higher level of w, which positively influences the number of migrant jobseekers; an increase in the number of migrant workers also increases the level of job vacancies (Equations (m.8.2.3) and (m.8.2.2)). Thus, the sharp decline in matching efficiencies during the late 1990s described in Chapter 6, which did not recover during the sample period, could be one of the key factors that has led to the high unemployment rate in China.

Influence of job destruction shocks, λ

If we increase λ by one standard deviation in the simulation, as Table 8.4 shows, dU increases significantly. In fact, λ^{ex} has two contrasting effects. On one hand, according to Equation (m.8.6), job destruction enlarges unemployment inflows. On the other hand, a higher job destruction rate leads to higher matching efficiency in the labor market, a (Equation (m.8.1.3)), which increases the job creation rate (Equation (m.8.2.1)). This simulation result indicates that the overall effect is an unambiguous increase in dU. In our sample period (1996–2008), the job destruction rate increased sharply after 1996, peaking in 1998, contributing to the jump in unemployment that coincided with China's SOE reforms.

Influence of job-search services, je

The presented results show that an increase in je lowers dU because the growth in je increases matching efficiency, thereby directly leading to new hires (Equations (m.8.1.3) and (m.8.1.4)). Further, increased matching efficiency also contributes to job creation, which further leads to a greater number of new hires (Equations (m.8.2.1), (m.8.2.2), and (m.8.1.2)). In addition, a higher θ also increases wages, leading to more migration, which in turn enlarges job creation, V (Equations (m.8.5) and (m.8.2.2)). Thus, providing more job-search services could be a good way to solve China's unemployment problem.

Influence of productivity, p

A higher level of p can contribute to both job creation and job destruction in China, as discussed earlier (Equations (8.2.1) and (8.3)). Simulations help us understand the total effect of p on unemployment. If we increase labor productivity by one standard deviation (approximately 36.2%), dU increases by 35.8%, indicating that a higher productivity level could lead to more urban unemployment.

However, the simulation results of all endogenous factors indicate that productivity might not be the most important factor in unemployment. In fact, the effect of raising the productivity level is stronger on job creation (24.5%) than it is on job destruction (14.3%), as shown in Table 8.5. The major problem is the inefficient process of turning vacant jobs into filled positions because of the low efficiency of job–worker matching.

In summary, improving matching efficiency and providing more job-search services could be important approaches to decrease unemployment and reduce the aggravating effects of job destruction and productivity growth. Further, with the help of the BC, the simulation results presented herein explain the shifts in China's U-V curve, which we will discuss in Section 8.5.

8.5   Dynamic Path of the U-V Curve and Shifts in the BC

8.5.1 The actual path of the U-V curve

By using data on unemployed workers and job vacancies, China's historical U-V curve for the 1996–2008 period can be obtained (see Fig. 8.1).

Fig. 8.1 China's historical U-V curve

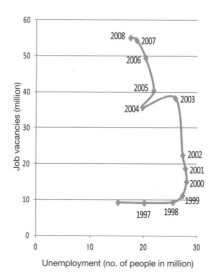

Source: NBS (1997–2009a).

Note: Unemployment includes both those who register at government offices and the laid-off workers excluded from the government's official unemployment statistics.

As shown in Fig. 8.1, the U-V curve first moved horizontally rightward during the 1996–1999 period, then turned upward around 2000, and gradually began to move back towards the upper left in 2001. The actual U-V curve is related to the shift in the BC and JC, which together determine the steady-state equilibrium of unemployment and job vacancies in the U-V space (Pissarides, 2000). The BC of China is obtained from Equations (m.8.6) and (m.1.2), with $\dot{U} = 0$. As discussed in Section 8.3.3, the coefficients of S_{it}^e / S_{it} and S_{it}^m / S_{it} are insignificant, and as employed jobseekers and migrant jobseekers do not cause congestion for unemployed workers, we reject these two terms. The result is as follows:

$$(L^{RE} - U) - \frac{a^u}{\lambda} U^{0.53} V^{0.23} + \frac{(B - D)}{\lambda} = 0, \tag{8.7}$$

which can be rewritten as a function in the U-V space:

$$V^{0.23} = \frac{1}{U^{0.53}} (\frac{\lambda}{a^u})[(L^{RE} - U) + \frac{(B - D)}{\lambda}]. \tag{8.8}$$

As a result, the BC in the U-V space is convex to the origin, and the BC shifts are determined by the ratio of λ / a^u and the labor force of urban residents, L^{RE}.[5] In the U-V space, the JC can be written as

$$V = \theta(U + 2.06S^e + 2.06S^m). \tag{8.9}$$

Therefore, in the U-V space, the JC is a line that has a slope of θ and an intercept of $(2.06S^e + 2.06S^m)\theta$.

8.5.2 Shifts in the BC and JC

During the first sub-period in our study, namely 1996–2000, the redundancy program in China led to a large degree of job destruction. The main redundancy program slowed around 2001, and exogenous job destruction shocks dropped to a low level between 2001 and 2008. The changes in matching efficiencies and other factors during 1996–2008 are graphically represented in Fig. 8.2.

---

5. Because $(B - D)$ is much smaller than L^{RE}, the influence of $(B - D)/\lambda$ is slight enough to be omitted here.

Fig. 8.2 Annual changes in a, λ, a/λ, θ, P, S^e, S^m and L^{RE}

(a) Changes in matching efficiency, a

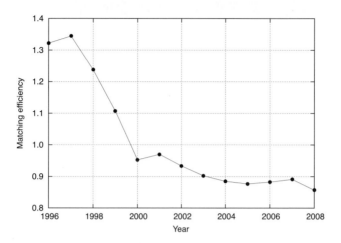

(b) Changes in job destruction rate, λ

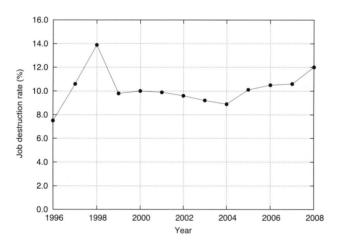

(c) Changes in $\dfrac{a}{\lambda}$

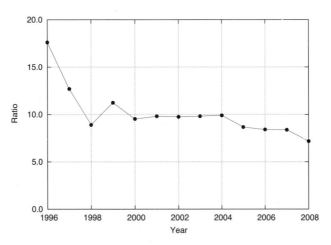

(d) Changes in market tightness, θ

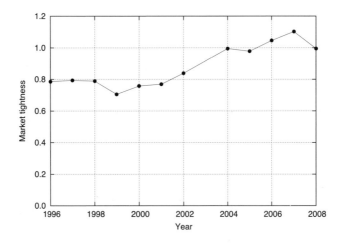

(e) Changes in labor productivity, p

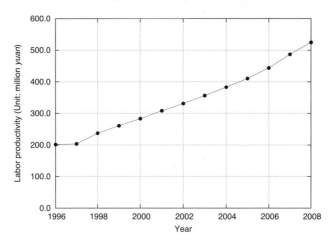

(f) Changes in the numbers of employed jobseekers, S^e, and migrant jobseekers, S^m

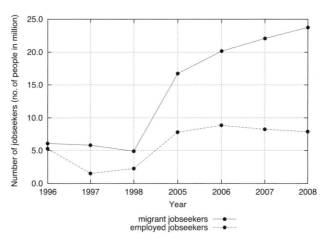

(g) Changes in labor force of urban residents, L^{RE}

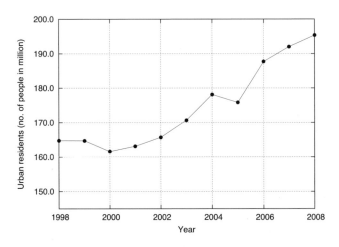

Sources: NBS (1997-2009a) and NBS (1997-2009b).

In the period 1996–2000, denoted as E1 and E2 in Fig. 8.3, the BC shifted outward largely because of the sharp increases in job destruction, λ, (Fig. 8.2(b)) and decreases in a / λ (Fig. 8.2(c)). Compared with the great jump in the BC, the movement of the JC is slight and can be ignored. For the second period, 2001–2008, we denote the mechanisms as E2 to E5 in Fig. 8.3. Since the SOE redundancy program ended in 2001, the job destruction rate, λ, declined during the period. However, the BC did not move backward since the low level of a / λ continued (Fig. 8.2(c)) because matching efficiency, a, declined significantly, as shown in Fig. 8.2(a). As long as matching efficiency remains at a low level, the BC cannot move back to its previous level and the unemployment problem will continue. Further, during the period 2001–2008, the urban labor force increased, as shown in Fig. 8.2(g), shifting the BC slightly outward.

For the JC, because the number of migrant jobseekers, S^m, and employed jobseekers, S^e, increased during 2001–2008, the JC moved upward. Moreover, the growth in productivity further moved the JC anticlockwise. Therefore, the equilibrium could move along the E2–E3–E4–E5 path, which is consistent with the actual historical U-V curve of China shown in Fig. 8.1.

Fig. 8.3 Shifts in the BC and JC

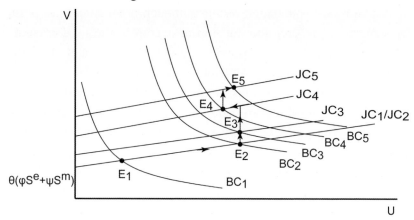

8.6   Conclusions

The coexistence of high unemployment and a high number of job vacancies in China has drawn much attention. In this chapter, we examined this issue using econometric models in a search and matching approach. We found a good fit of this theory to China's actual situation, which indicates that the country has made strong progress in its transition towards a market economy. However, labor-market frictions, which cannot be avoided in a market economy, are serious and could be the most important reason for the high rate of unemployment in urban China.

To examine the determinants of urban unemployment, we constructed an econometric model that comprised job–worker matching, job creation and destruction, unemployment evolution, and migrant and employed worker job searches. The findings with regard to China's labor market are fivefold. First, we found that productivity, interest rate, market tightness and job agencies significantly influence the determination of job creation and destruction as well as the behavior of jobseekers, which indicates that the labor market has rapidly developed in urban China. Second, the country's high unemployment rate is caused not only by high job destruction but also by low job–worker matching efficiency. In the 2000s, in particular, when large-scale job destruction in the SOE sector gradually ceased and numerous jobs in the private sector were created, the main cause for unemployment was the low efficiency of job–worker matching.

Third, productivity growth may also contribute to unemployment, as indicated by our simulation results; although productivity has positive effects on both job creation and job destruction, the jobs created by productivity gains do not efficiently lead to employment. Therefore, the problem of low matching efficiency remains. Fourth, an increase in rural–urban migration does not lead to urban unemployment: an increase in migrant jobseekers neither reduces the number of new hires from unemployed jobseekers, given a certain number of job vacancies, nor increases market tightness for unemployed workers, because of adequate job creation in China. Thus, as long as job creation is sufficiently active, limiting rural–urban migration is unnecessary for tackling the urban unemployment problem. Fifth, the presented model confirmed that providing job-search services is an effective way to reduce the unemployment rate in China, as it not only improves market efficiency but also encourages job creation.

Finally, we used the shifts in the BC and JC to explain the U-V changes in urban China. The shocks of the redundancy program in the 1990s shifted the BC outward, but even when these shocks disappeared in the 2000s, the BC did not move backward because of a drop in matching efficiency. Further, in the 2000s, an increase in the number of non-unemployed jobseekers shifted the JC upward, which avoided worsening China's unemployment issue.

To the best of our knowledge, this study is the first of its kind to use the search and matching model to solve the unemployment problem in China. An appealing avenue for further research could thus be examination of the individual-level behaviors of job-search and labor-market outcomes in China.

Appendix 8A Details of estimation results

Table 8.6 Estimation results of the unemployment model

Dep. Var.: a_{it}	Model	Comparison	Dep. Var.: a_{it}^u	Model	Comparison
Var.	3SLS	SUR	Var.	3SLS	SUR
Δp_{it}	-2.31×10^{-5}	-2.41×10^{-5}	Δp_{it}	-8.42×10^{-5}	-7.98×10^{-5}
	[–5.11]***	[–5.49]***		[–7.27]***	[–7.18]***
je_{it}	0.13	0.09	je_{it}	0.08	–0.02
	[5.20]***	[4.00]***		[1.29]	[–0.28]
λ_{it}	0.79	1.25	λ_{it}	–4.49	–5.39
	[2.97]**	[4.87]***		[–6.59]***	[–8.30]***
Const.	0.77	0.82	Const.	1.00	1.22
	[13.25]***	[14.33]***		[6.66]***	[8.37]***
R	0.72	0.72	R.	0.62	0.61
Adj. R	0.70	0.69	Adj. R.	0.58	0.57
N	342	341	N.	346	345

Dep. Var.: $(p_{it}-w_{it})$	Model	Comparison	Dep. Var.: w_{it}	Model	Comparison
Var.	3SLS	SUR	Var.	3SLS	SUR
"c"	0.76	0.003	"β"	0.26	0.34
	[4.98]***	[0.09]		[12.69]***	[29.19]***
			"c"	0.76	0.003
				[4.98]***	[0.09]
Const.	11806.75	16979.06	Const.	5175.97	4635.73
	[4.13]***	[5.73]***		[5.05]***	[6.70]***
R	0.91	0.88	R.	0.71	0.84
Adj. R	0.87	0.84	Adj. R.	0.68	0.83
N	104	104	N.	339	368

Note: "c" and "β" are estimated values for c and β respectively.

Table 8.6 (continued)

Dep. Var.: λ_{it}	Model	Comparison
Var.	3SLS	SUR
p_{it}	6.93×10^{-7}	8.23×10^{-7}
	[4.94]***	[8.15]***
θ_{it}	0.07	0.01
	[1.60]	[1.38]
Const.	−0.01	0.02
	[−0.59]	[2.36]**
R	0.11	0.24
Adj. R	0.07	0.21
N	342	369

Dep. Var.: S_{it}^{e}	Model	Comparison	Dep. Var.: S_{it}^{m}	Model	Comparison
Var.	3SLS	SUR	Var.	3SLS	SUR
$\log \lambda_{it}$	0.24	0.10	$\log \lambda_{it}$	−0.27	−0.17
	[1.40]	[0.69]		[−0.59]	[−1.88]
$\log p_{it}$	0.84	1.57	$\log p_{it}$	−0.07	0.20
	[3.65]***	[8.92]***		[−0.09]	[0.59]
$\log \theta_{it}$	−1.96	—	$\log \theta_{it}$	2.12	—
	[−1.51]	—		[0.79]	—
$\log je_{it}$	0.06	0.03	$\log je_{it}$	0.62	0.16
	[0.44]	[0.22]		[1.89]*	[1.10]
$\log E_{it}$	0.98	0.80	$\log w_{it}$	1.22	0.96
	[6.34]***	[8.08]***		[2.21]**	[3.46]***
Const.	−13.48	−19.67	Const.	−9.51	−9.51
	[−4.87]***	[−9.14]***		[−2.27]**	[−7.40]***
R	0.61	0.60	R	0.72	0.78
Adj. R	0.59	0.58	Adj. R	0.63	0.74
N	156	182	N	132	190

Note: *p < 0.1, **p < 0.05, ***p < 0.01

Conclusion

Over the past two decades, China's urban labor market has shared many common behaviors with a mature market, which has enabled us to obtain significant results using a framework of modern structural econometric models. These models have allowed us to answer the three research questions posed in Chapter 1. Moreover, the results of these models explain three important issues in China's urban labor market: the real determinants of urban unemployment, the imperfectness of China's urban labor market, and how rural-urban migration affects the urban labor market. We discuss these three issues in this concluding chapter.

Determinants of Urban Unemployment

Starting from the usual concerns of labor supply and demand, we found that the disequilibrium between the supply and demand of urban resident workers arises from wage rigidity, which keeps the average level of resident wages above market-clearing wages (1.57 times higher on average, with a standard deviation of 0.34 for all observations). This leads to a gap between labor supply and demand, which causes unemployment, as discussed in Chapter 3. The resident wage level cannot react to the unemployment rate effectively owing to the imperfectness of the resident labor market.

However, unemployment cannot be attributed solely to imbalances between labor supply and demand. In recent years, large-scale job and worker reallocations have characterized the labor market in China, as described in Chapter 5. Such degree of reallocation has increased labor-market frictions, extending the time needed for workers to search for jobs that fit their requirements and skills, and for firms to approach potential employees (Cahuc and Zylberberg 2004). We captured this process in the matching models presented in Chapter 6, finding that the matching efficiency of China's urban labor market declined greatly in the late 1990s and remained at a low level in the 2000s. This trend helps explain why the high unemployment rate in China does not fall even though there are a large number of job vacancies. Search and matching theory therefore provides a suitable modeling framework to study this issue.

Under the search and matching approach, changes in unemployment depend on unemployment inflows and outflows. The decline in matching efficiency in China affects the outflows from unemployment, as modeled in Chapter 8. It not only reduces new hires for a given number of job vacancies, but also negatively affects job creation. The reason for this trend is that the present discounted value of the expected profit from a job vacancy decreases when matching efficiency declines, which discourages firms from creating new job positions, as discussed in Chapter 7. In addition, lower matching efficiency also reduces the positive effects of migration on job creation by reducing average wages in urban areas, making it less attractive to work in large cities. Specifically, the presented simulations indicate that a small decrease in matching efficiency leads to an increase in unemployment growth considerably.

Inflows into unemployment comprise workers who are fired or laid off owing to the destruction of jobs. In China, the exogenous shock of job destruction, due to enterprise reforms and worker retrenchment policies, leads to large inflows into unemployment. Indeed, our simulation results in Chapter 8 show that an increase in job destruction by 80% worsens unemployment changes by 104% (see Table 8.4).

Finally, China's productivity has grown throughout the past two decades, which is a permanent change rather than a temporary shock. We found that productivity positively influences both job creation and endogenous job destruction in China. The positive effect on job creation, termed the capitalization effect, arises because higher productivity increases profits and thus encourages firms to create more jobs. However, productivity growth also positively affects job destruction, termed creative destruction, based on rapid technological advancement. Although our simulation results show that the effect of the rising productivity level is stronger on job creation than it is on job destruction, it still increases unemployment, because only a proportion of job vacancies are successfully filled by workers owing to low matching efficiency in the labor market.

Previous empirical studies have often divided exogenous shocks into *reallocation shocks* and *aggregate shocks*. Reallocation shocks refer to the restructuring of production units and are akin to changes in matching functions or the job destruction rate, which shift the BC. By contrast, aggregate shocks mainly refer to productivity growth and the increase in the number of non-unemployed jobseekers, which shift the JC upward in our model (Cahuc and Zylberberg 2004). Further, in a long-run stationary equilibrium, reallocation shocks are marked by movements in unemployment and vacancies in the same direction, whereas aggregate shocks are characterized by contrasting movements in these two variables (Cahuc and Zylberberg 2004).

Thus, the rapidly increasing unemployment rate in China in the late 1990s was mainly caused by reallocation shocks (including exogenous job destruction and declining matching efficiency), with a large outward shift in the BC. After 2002, exogenous job destruction shocks disappeared, but the BC did not shift back to its original position because a continued low level of matching efficiency made it impossible for an immediate reduction in unemployment. Simultaneously, positive aggregate shocks, such as an increase in the number of migrant jobseekers and productivity growth, shifted the JC upward, which increased job vacancies and gradually decreased unemployment after 2002.

The Imperfectness of China's Urban Labor Market

The causes of unemployment in urban China indicate the existence of an imperfect labor market. Although China's labor market has developed significantly since the economic revolution in 1978, some influences of the planned economy remain. Further, increased job and worker reallocations require more complete information, but China's related institutions are not yet efficient enough because of its status as a developing labor market.

First, the rigidity of the average wages of urban residents is a result of the wage system in SOEs. It is difficult to reduce wages even if SOEs are loss-making (Xiao 2007), as the senior management teams of most such enterprises are recruited by the government; therefore, they care about political returns and personal gains rather than firm profits (Tang 2010). Although most private enterprises pay feasible wages, the situation in SOEs has changed little and their rigid wages remain a large obstacle towards the formation of a perfect labor market.

Second, imperfect information, which causes frictions in the labor market, suggests ineffective labor market functioning in China. Before the urban labor market began to develop in the early 1980s, workers were generally posted administratively, and most firms did not have the right to decide on hiring. With the transition to a market economy, a real labor market developed, but its functioning has not yet been fully implemented. Most recruitment activities and job searches are carried out by job agencies, but the quality of job services and efficiency of job exchanges remain low. Several studies have already pointed out issues such as low efficiency in operating job agencies, shortage of staff, low skills, etc. (see Zhao and Li 2005; Li and Qiu 2010). The less developed function of China's labor exchanges has thus been an obstacle to reduction in labor-market frictions.

Third, the household registration system leads to the regional segmentation of the labor market. Although the scale of worker reallocation is large in China, worker mobility occurs mostly within the same provinces, or arises because of short-term rural–urban migration. The flow of skilled workers between provinces is small, because the household registration system prevents workers from finding permanent jobs outside their home provinces, leading to mismatches and reduced efficiency. Job-search services in many cities also give priority to jobseekers who are included in the local household registration (*Hukou*); in particular, the services for unemployed workers are limited to local residents. Further, some permanent jobs, especially those in SOEs, are limited to or allotted on a priority basis to locals. For instance, a survey reported that over 60% of jobseekers consider household registration to be an obstacle to their search for work.[1] The direct result of this household registration system is regional segmentation of the labor market, leading to geographic mismatches and reduced matching efficiency. For instance, the Human Resources Market Information Monitoring Center in China reported that in the fourth quarter of 2010, the number of applications for equipment assembly jobs in Jinan city was twice the number of job vacancies, whereas similar applications in

---

1. "*Guanzhu hukou: qiye yongren pianhao bendi, hukou hai shi dao kan ma*" (Priority to local residents in firm recruitment: Is household registration still an obstacle?), http://edu.sina.com.cn/l/2004-10-20/88738.html.

Shenyang city were only one-third of the number of job vacancies.[2] These mismatches will remain as long as the household registration system still plays an important role in the labor market in China.

Consequently, China's labor market is highly imperfect, reducing the efficiency of market functioning and increasing the unemployment rate. Although labor market imperfectness in developed countries that have mature labor markets also remains because of unions' bargaining power, minimum wages, etc., these factors provide important socioeconomic benefits, such as reducing earnings differences. By contrast, the imperfectness of China's labor market has few benefits and actually leads to serious problems.

How does Rural–Urban Migration Affect Urban Labor Markets?

Rural migrants are often blamed for taking away jobs from urban residents. However, under strict structural econometric analysis, we found that rural–urban migration does not contribute to urban unemployment in China. Our model in Chapter 4 showed that although rural migrants can substitute urban residents in conditional labor demand, their lower wages increase output, thereby increasing overall demand for resident workers. Indeed, the presented simulations showed that the latter positive impact is greater than the former substitution effect in China, namely migrants lead to the creation of more jobs for residents than they take away.

The effect of rural–urban migration in China was also confirmed using the search and matching approach in Chapters 6 and 8. First, the matching function estimations did not show strong evidence that migrants compete with residents for jobs. Second, regarding unemployment changes with endogenous job creation, we found that an increase in the number of migrants does not influence market tightness (defined as the ratio of job vacancies to jobseekers). This finding occurs because when there are more migrants in the urban labor market, profit maximization encourages firms to create more jobs to meet this increase in the number of jobseekers. This level of job creation is sufficient in the current situation of high economic growth in China.

---

2. China's Employment, http://www.lm.gov.cn/.

Rural–urban migration has been an inevitable trend in China. Unlike the situation in developed countries, internal migration serves as a rational approach to resource reallocation that benefits the national economy. In the early stages of development, governments often invest heavily in urban areas and adopt a "price scissors" policy between agricultural goods and industrial goods. As a result, capital endowments become particularly concentrated in urban areas and rural–urban migration becomes necessary for filling the consequent increase in urban labor demand.

Incidentally, rural immigrants are a group of unskilled workers that flow into urban areas for work. Theoretically, in a perfect market, the migration of unskilled workers would reduce the wages of unskilled residents, as observed in many developed countries (Cahuc and Zylberberg 2004). However, migration has not affected the wages of urban residents in China because of the segmentation of the labor market and the rigidity of resident wages.

The findings of our models might be helpful in the context of the current internal migration policies in China. Note that the situation could change in the future if the country's economic growth reaches the stage that the capital and resources in urban areas become inadequate for greater job creation; if that were to happen, rural–urban migration would definitely lead to higher levels of urban unemployment.

Overall Conclusion

In conclusion, our study suggests that in order to develop the labor market in China, policies to increase wage flexibility, job–worker matching efficiency, and labor mobility are needed. Potential policies to ameliorate the situation include reducing the state's monopolistic power, providing more job-search services, and relaxing internal migration restrictions. We hope that this study contributes to an increased awareness of the status of China's labor market and helps reduce the problems of unemployment, the rising income gap, and urban poverty, in order to promote nationwide economic development. Note that this study focused on the urban labor market and inflows of rural migrants to urban areas. Further studies could involve the rural labor market, migration decisions, and firms' job creation opportunities in rural China.

List of First Sources

The author would like to thank the following journals for granting permission to reuse the following articles in this book:

Liu, Y. 2011a. Labor market matching with heterogeneous job seekers in China. *Economics Bulletin*, 31 (3): 1980–92.

Liu, Y. 2011b. An econometric model of disequilibrium unemployment in urban China. *Toukeigaku [Statistics]*, 101: 17–29.

Liu, Y. 2012b. Does internal immigration always lead to urban unemployment in emerging economies? A structural approach based on data from China. *Hitotsubashi Journal of Economics*, 53 (1): 85–105.

Liu, Y. 2013a. Labor market matching and unemployment in urban China. *China Economic Review*, 24: 108–128.

Liu, Y. 2013b. Job and worker reallocation in China: Trends and characteristics during 1991–2009. *The Chinese Economy*, 46 (5) (September/October 2013). Copyright © 2013 by M. E. Sharpe, Inc.

Bibliography

Anderson, P. M., and S. M. Burgess. 2000. Empirical matching functions: Estimation and interpretation using state-level data. *The Review of Economics and Statistics*, 82 (1): 93–102.

Appleton, S., J. Knight, L. Song, and Q. Xia. 2004. Contrasting paradigms: Segmentation and competitiveness in the formation of the Chinese labour market. *Journal of Chinese Economic and Business Studies*, 2 (3): 185–205.

Bai, Q., and T. Huang. 2010. *Dangqian woguo jiegou xing shiye de xian zhuang fenxi* [On the situation of the current structural unemployment in our country]. *Commercial Times*, 30: 8–9.

Bank of Japan (BOJ). 2008. *Tyuugoku roudou shijyou ni o ke ru roudouryoku idou to jyukyuu misumaxtuti no genjyou to tenbou* [Labor migration and demand-supply mismatch in China: The present state and prospects]. http://www.boj.or.jp/announcements/ release_2008/itaku0804a.pdf.

Bao, S., Ö. B. Bodvarsson, J. W. Hou, and Y. Zhao. 2009. The regulation of migration in a transition economy: China's hukou system. *IZA Discussion Paper*, No. 4493.

Barro, R. J., and X. Sala-i-Martin. 2004. *Economic Growth*. Cambridge, MA: MIT Press, 2th ed.

Blanchard, O. J., and P. Diamond. 1994. Ranking, unemployment duration, and wages. *Review of Economic Studies*, 61 (3): 417–34.

Blanchard, O. J., P. Diamond, R. E. Hall, and J. Yellen. 1989. The Beveridge curve. *Brookings Papers on Economic Activity*, 1: 1–76.

Bodvarsson, Ö. B., and J. W. Hou. 2010. The effects of aging on migration in a transition economy: The case of China. *IZA Discussion Paper*, No. 5070.

Broersma, L. 1997. Competition between employed and unemployed job searchers: Is there a difference between the UK and the Netherlands? *Applied Economics Letters*, 4 (3): 199–203.

Broersma, L., and J. C. Van Ours. 1999. Job searchers, job matches and the elasticity of matching. *Labour Economics*, 6 (1): 77–93.

Bulow, J., and L. H. Summers. 1986. A theory of dual labor markets with application to industrial policy, discrimination and Keynesian unemployment. *Journal of Labor Economics*, 4 (3): 376–414.

Burford, R. L. 1970. Internal migration in a developing economy: Case of Taiwan. *Annals of Regional Science*, 4 (2): 80–9.

Burgess, S. M. 1993. A model of competition between unemployed and employed job searchers: An application to the unemployment outflow rate in Britain. *The Economic Journal*, 103: 1190–1204.

Cahuc, P., and A. Zylberberg. 2004. *Labor Economics*. Cambridge, MA: MIT Press.

Cai, F., and Y. Du. 2007. *Green book of population and labor no. 8: The coming Lewisian turning point and its policy implications* [in Chinese]. China: Social Science Academic Press.

Cai, F., Y. Du, and M. Wang. 2010. *Green book of population and labor no. 11: Labor market challenges in the post-crisis era* [in Chinese]. China: Social Sciences Academic Press.

China Popin. May 2004. http://www.cpirc.org.cn/rdzt/rd_ldrk_detail. asp?id=3757.

Cole, W. E., and R. D. Sanders. 1985. Internal migration and urban employment in the third world. *The American Economic Review*, 75 (3): 481–94.

Coles, M. G., and E. Smith. 1996. Cross-section estimation of the matching function: Evidence from England and Wales. *Economica*, 63 (252): 589–97.

Dai, Z. 2010. *Pojie dangdai zhongguo shiye nanti de lixing sikao* [Rational consideration on solution of Chinese unemployment problem]. *Zhongguo Shangjie* [*Chinese Business*], 2010 (05): 283–284.

Davis, S. J., and J. C. Haltiwanger. 1992. Gross job creation, gross job destruction, and employment reallocation. *The Quarterly Journal of Economics*, 107 (3): 819–63.

Davis, S. J., and J. C. Haltiwanger. 1996. *Job Creation and Destruction*. Cambridge, MA and London: MIT Press.

Davis, S. J., and J. C. Haltiwanger. 1999. Gross job flows. In *Handbook of Labor Economics*, edited by O. Ashenfelter and D. E. Card. 2711–2805. Amsterdam: Elsevier Science, North-Holland.

De La Rupelle, M., Q. Deng, S. Li, and T. Vendryes. 2009. Land rights insecurity and temporary migration in rural China. *IZA Discussion Paper*, No. 4668.

Demurger, S., M. Gurgand, S. Li, and X. Yue. 2009. Migrants as second-class workers in urban China? A decomposition analysis. *Journal of Comparative Economics*, 37: 610–28.

Deng, H., R. H. McGuckin, J. Xu, Y. Liu, and Y. Liu. 2005. The dynamics of China's labor market: Job creation and destruction in the industrial sector. *East Asian Economic Perspectives*, 18: 58–92.

Destefanis, S., and R. Fonseca. 2007. Matching efficiency and labour market reform in Italy: A macroeconometric assessment. *Labour*, 21 (1): 57–84.

Diamond, P. A., and E. S. Maskin. 1979. An equilibrium analysis of search and breach of contract. *Bell Journal of Economics*, 10 (1): 282–316.

Dong, W. 2010. *Zhongguo shiye wenti de xianzhong yuanyin yu duice* [Situations, reasons, and solutions of unemployment problem in China]. *Xiandai Jingji Xinxi* [*Modern Economy Information*], 2010 (10): 171–172.

Fahr, R., and U. Sunde. 2005. Job and vacancy competition in empirical matching functions. *Labour Economics*, 12 (6): 773–80.

Fu, S., X. Dong, and G. Chai. 2010. Industry specialization, diversification, churning, and unemployment in Chinese cities. *China Economic Review*, 21 (4): 508–20.

General Office of the State Council of the People's Republic of China (GOSC). 2004. *Guowu yuan bangongting guanyu jinyibu zuohao gaishan nongmin jincheng jiuye huanjing gongzuo de tongzhi* [Circular of the General Office of the State Council on improving the job search environment of rural–urban migrants]. http://www.gov.cn/gongbao/content/2005/content_63333.htm.

Giles, J., A. Park, and J. Zhang. 2005. What is China's true unemployment rate? *China Economic Review*, 16 (2): 149–70.

Gong, X., S. T. Kong, S. Li, and X. Meng. 2008. Rural-urban migrants, a driving force for growth. In *China's Dilemma, Economic Growth, the Environment and Climate Change*, edited by L. Song, R. Garnaut, and W. Thye Woo. 110–52. Brookings Institution Press/ANU e-Press with Asia-Pacific Press.

Greene, W. H. 2008. *Econometric analysis*. Upper Saddle River, NJ: Prentice Hall, 6th ed.

Guanzhu hukou: Qiye yongren pianhao bendi, hukou hai shi dao kan ma [Priority to local residents in firm recruitment: Is household registration still an obstacle?] http://edu.sina.com.cn/l/2004-10-20/88738.html.

Hamermesh, D. S., W. H. J. Hassink, and J. C. Van Ours. 1996. Job turnover and labor turnover: A taxonomy of employment dynamics. *Annales d'Economie et de Statistique*, 34 (3): 1264–92.

Han, J. 2008. *Laodong hetong fa shishi dui minying qiye laodong guanxi de yingxiang* [Influences of the law of employment contracts on labor relations in private enterprises]. *Special Zoon Economy*, April: 151–3.

Harris, J. R., and M. P. Todaro. 1970. Migration, unemployment, and development: A two-sector analysis. *American Economic Review*, 60 (1): 126–42.

Huang, N., and X. Wang. 2010. Research on the relationship between migrant workers and urban workers based on a model of heterogeneous productive factors [in Chinese]. *Wuhan University Journal (Philosophy and Social Sciences)*, 3: 464–8.

Hynninen, S. M. 2009. Heterogeneity of job seekers in labour market matching. *Applied Economics Letters*, 16 (18): 1819–23.

Ibourk, A., B. Maillardb, S. Perelmanc, and H. R. Sneessens. 2004. Aggregate matching efficiency: A stochastic production frontier approach. *Empirica*, 31 (1): 1–25.

Kanamori, T., and Z. Zhao. 2004. Private sector development in the People's Republic of China. *Asian Development Bank Economics Working Paper*, No. 237.

Kangasharju, A., J. Pehkonen, and S. Pekkala. 2005. Returns to scale in a matching model: Evidence from disaggregated panel data. *Applied Economics*, 37 (1): 115–8.

Kano, S., and M. Ohta. 2005. Estimating a matching function and regional matching efficiencies: Japanese panel data for 1973–1999. *Japan and the World Economy*, 17 (1): 25–41.

Knight, J., and S. Li. 2006. Unemployment duration and earnings of re-employed workers in urban China. *China Economic Review*, 17 (2): 103–19.

Knight, J., and L. Song. 2005. *Towards a Labor Market in China*. Oxford: Oxford University Press.

Knight, J., L. Song, and H. Jia. 1999. Chinese rural migrants in urban enterprises: Three perspectives. *Journal of Development Studies*, 35 (3): 73–104.

Knight, J., and J. Xie. 2006. How high is urban unemployment in China? *Journal of Chinese Economic and Business Studies*, 4 (2): 91–107.

Knight, J., and L. Yueh, 2004. Urban insiders versus rural outsiders: Complementarity or competition in China's urban labour market? In *Economics Series Working Papers*, 217. Oxford: University of Oxford, Department of Economics.

Knight, J., and L. Yueh, 2009. Segmentation or competition in China's urban labour market? *Cambridge Journal of Economics*, 33 (1): 79–94.

Lagarde, S., E. Maurin, and C. Torelli. 1995. *Flows of Workers and Job Reallocation*. Mimeo, Insee: Direction des Statistiques Demographiques et Sociales.

Lewis, A. W. 1954. Economic development with unlimited supplies of labour. *Manchester School of Economic and Social Studies*, 22 (2): 139–91.

Li, C. 1996. Surplus rural laborers and internal migration in China. *Asian Survey*, 36 (11): 1122–45.

Li, C., and W. Qiu. 2010. *Tisheng gonggong zhiye jieshao jigou jiuye fuwu nengli yanjiu-yi Beijing weili* [Improving services in job exchanges: A case study of Beijing]. *Inquiry into Economic Issues*, 2: 174–178.

Li lv li ci tiao zheng yi lang [A list of interest rate adjustments (by the Central Bank of China)]. http://data.eastmoney.com/cjsj/yhll.html.

Li, X. 2003. *Renli ziyuan zhongjie zuzhi yu zhongjie shichang de fazhan* [Development of human resource intermediaries and job agencies]. *Nankai Business Review*: 25–30.

Li, X., and J. Li. 2007. An analysis of the unemployment problem in China using the Beveridge curve [in Chinese]. *Northwest Population Journal*, 28 (2): 1–7.

Li, Y., Z. Zhang, and T. Huang. 2001. *Zhongguo chengzhen jiuye yanjiu [A study of urban employment in China]*. China: China Planning Press.

Lin, Y., and Z. Zhang. 2011. *Nongmingong de liangbumen shengcun: Laodongli zhuanyi yu jiating liushou beilun de zhidu kaocha.* [Life of rural migrants: A study of labor transfers and left-behind families]. *Theory Journal*, 2: 58–61.

Lindeboom, M., J. C. Van Ours, and G. Renes. 1994. Matching employers and workers: An empirical analysis on the effectiveness of search. *Oxford Economic Papers*, 46: 45–67.

Liu, Q. 2012. Unemployment and labor force participation in urban China. *China Economic Review*, 23 (1): 18–33.

Liu, Y. 2010. Immigration contribution and a model of inner-city dual labor market: An econometric study based on panel data from China. *Kyoto University Economic Society Monograph*, No. 201012206.

Liu, Y. 2011a. Labor market matching with heterogeneous job seekers in China. *Economics Bulletin*, 31 (3): 1980–92.

Liu, Y. 2011b. An econometric model of disequilibrium unemployment in urban China. *Toukeigaku [Statistics]*, 101: 17–29.

Liu, Y. 2011c. Determinants of unemployment dynamics and the Beveridge Curve in China: Econometric models using the search and matching approach. *Kyoto University Economic Society Monograph*, No. 201108220.

Liu, Y. 2012a. Reduced-form estimation of matching function in the Chinese labor Market [in Japanese]. *Tokegaku [Statistics]*, 102: 105-113.

Liu, Y. 2012b. Does internal immigration always lead to urban unemployment in emerging economies? A structural approach based on data from China. *Hitotsubashi Journal of Economics*, 53 (1): 85-105.

Liu, Y. 2013a. Labor market matching and unemployment in urban China. *China Economic Review*, 24: 108-128.

Liu, Y. 2013b. Job and worker reallocation in China: Trends and characteristics during 1991–2009. *The Chinese Economy*, 46 (5) (September/October 2013).

Liu, Yi. 2010. *Butong huji laodongli de chengzhen jiuye jihui yu shouru chayi* [Employment and wage gap between the labor groups of different household registration]. In *Zhongguo Laodongli Shichang: Qianjing, Wenti, Yu Duice* [China's Labor Market: Prospects, Problems, and Solutions], edited by Z. Xiao. 327–45. China: Nankai University Press.

Mankiw, G. N. 2000. *Macroeconomics*. US: Worth Publishers, 4th ed.

Mas-Colell, A., M. D. Whinston, and J. R. Green. 1995. *Microeconomic Theory*. Oxford: Oxford University Press.

McCall, J. J. 1970. Economics of information and job search. *Quarterly Journal of Economics*, 84 (1): 113–26.

Meng, F. 2010. *Chengshi zhigong yu nongmingong gongzi shouru chayi ji yuanyin fenxi — yi Beijing shi laodongli gongzi shouru wei li* [Determinants of the wage differences between urban residents and rural migrants: Based on a survey from Beijing]. *Price Theory and Practice*, 2: 37–8.

Meng, X., and D. Zhang. 2010. Labour market impact of large scale internal migration on Chinese urban 'native' workers. *IZA Discussion Paper*, No. 5288.

Meng, X., and J. Zhang. 2001. The two-tier labor market in urban China: Occupational segregation and wage differentials between urban residents and rural migrants in Shanghai. *Journal of Comparative Economics*, 29: 485–504.

Ministry of Finance People's Republic of China (MOF). 2002. *Caizheng bu guojia shuiwu zongju guanyu xiagang shiye renyuan zaijiu ye youguan shuishou zhengce wenti de tongzhi* [Circular of the State Administration of Taxation, Ministry of Finance on the tax policy of unemployed and laid-off workers]. http://shui.falvba.net/Article/558.html.

Ministry of Labor of the People's Republic of China (MOL). 1992. *Guanyu 1993 nian qi pubian shixing dongtai tiaokong de laodong gongzi jihua de tongzhi* [The State Council notice for practicing dynamic-controlled flexible wages from 1993]. http://law. 51labour.com/lawshow-49689. html.

Mortensen, D. T. 1986. Job search and labor market analysis. In *Handbook of Labor Economics*, edited by O. Ashenfelter and R. Layard. 849–919. Amsterdam: Elsevier Science, North-Holland.

Mortensen, D. T., and C. A. Pissarides. 1999. New developments in models of search in the labor market. In *Handbook of Labor Economics*, edited by O. Ashenfelter and D. E. Card. 2567–2627. Amsterdam: Elsevier Science, North-Holland.

Mumford, K., and P. N. Smith. 1999. The hiring function reconsidered: On closing the circle. *Oxford Bulletin of Economics and Statistics*, 61 (3): 343–64.

National Bureau of Statistics of China (NBS). 1993–2010a. *China Labor Statistical Yearbook 1993–2011*. China: China Statistics Press.

National Bureau of Statistics of China (NBS). 1993–2010b. *China Statistical Yearbook 1993–2011*. China: China Statistics Press.

National Bureau of Statistics of China (NBS). 2005–2010c. *China Population Statistics Yearbook 2005–2009*. China: China Statistics Press.

National Bureau of Statistics of China (NBS). 2005–2008d. *China Yearbook of Rural Household Survey 2005–2009*. China: China Statistics Press.

National Bureau of Statistics of China (NBS). 2011a. National accounting reporting system [in Chinese]. http://www.stats.gov.cn/tjzd/gjtjzd/t20110506_402723992.htm.

National Bureau of Statistics of China (NBS). 2011b Labor statistics reporting system [in Chinese]. http://www.stats.gov.cn/tjzd/gjtjzd/t20110506_402724083.htm.

Ning, Z., Z. Wang, H. Zhang, and W. Fang. 2005. Economics explanation on overstaffed and rigid-wage monopoly government [in Chinese], *Modern Economic Science*, 1.

OECD. 1996. *Employment Outlook*. Paris: OECD.

Ottaviana, G. I. P., and G. Peri. Forthcoming. Rethinking the effects of immigration on wages. *The Journal of the European Economic Association*.

Petrongolo, B., and C. A. Pissarides. 2001. Looking into the black box: A survey of the matching function. *Journal of Economic Literature*, 39 (2): 390–431.

Phan, D., and I. Coxhead. 2010. Inter-provincial migration and inequality during Vietnam's transition. *Journal of Development Economics*, 91 (1): 100–12.

Piore, M. J. 1980. Economic fluctuation, job security, and labor market duality in Italy, France, and the United States. *Politics and Society*, 9 (4): 379–407.

Pissarides, C. A. 1979. Job matchings with state employment agencies and random search. *Economic Journal*, 89 (356): 818–33.

Pissarides, C. A. 1986. Unemployment and vacancies in Britain. *Economic Policy*, 1 (3): 499–559.

Pissarides, C. A. 2000. *Equilibrium Unemployment Theory*. Cambridge, MA: MIT Press, 2nd ed.

Renbaobu fubuzhang Yang, Zhiming: Tanxing gongzi jidai wanshan [A flexible wage systems need to be completed quickly: Said by Zhiming Yang, the Vice-minister of Ministry of Human Resources and Social Security of the People's Republic of China]. http://news.sohu. com/20090922/n266894500.shtml.

Research Office of the State Council (ROSC). 2006. *Zhongguo Nongmingong Diaoyan Baogao* [Research Report on the Rural–Urban Migrant Workers of China]. China: China Yanshi Press.

Rogerson, R., R. Shimer, and R. Wright. 2005. Search-theoretic models of the labor market: A survey. *Journal of Economic Literature*, XLIII: 959–88.

Romer, D. 2005. *Advanced Macroeconomics*. Boston: McGraw-Hill/Irwin, 3rd ed.

Rozelle, S., J. E. Taylor, and A. DeBrauw. 1999. Migration, remittances, and agricultural productivity in China. *The American Economic Review*, 89 (2): 287–91.

Saint-Paul, G. 1996. *Dual Labor Markets: A Macroeconomic Perspective*. Cambridge, MA: MIT Press.

Samson, L. 1994. The Beveridge curve and regional disparities in Canada. *Applied Economics*, 26 (10): 937–47.

Sasaki, M. 2008. Matching function for the Japanese labor market: Random or stockflow? *Bulletin of Economic Research*, 60 (2): 209–30.

Sjöholm, F. 2010. Will science and technology solve China's unemployment problem? *Asian Economic Papers*, 9 (2): 1–28.

State Administration of Taxation (SAT). 2001–2008. *Tax Yearbook of China 2001–2008*. China: China Tax Publishing House.

State Information Center, Statistical Database of China Economic Information Network (CEInet). http://www.cei.gov.cn.

Stiglitz, J. E. 1974. Alternative theories of wage determination and unemployment in LDC's: The labor turnover model. *The Quarterly Journal of Economics*, 88 (2): 194–227.

Sun, M., and C. C. Fan. 2011. China's permanent and temporary migrants: Differentials and changes, 1990-2000. *The Professional Geographer*, 63 (1): 92–112.

Sunde, U. 2007. Empirical matching functions: Searchers, vacancies, and (un-)biased elasticities. *Economica*, 74 (295): 537–60.

Tang, L. 2010. *Guoyou qiye gongzi zhidu gaige de huigu yu sikao* [Changes in the wage system in state-owned enterprises]. *Special Zone Economy*, June: 116–118.

Tian, S. 2010. Changes in the status of rural migrant workers in the urban labor market [in Chinese]. *China Business and Market*, 12: 66–9.

Todaro, M. P. 1969. A model for labor migration and urban unemployment in less developed countries. *The American Economic Review*, 59 (1): 138 –48.

Todaro, M. P., and S. C. Smith. 2003. *Economic development*. New York: Addison Wesley, 8th ed.

Van Ours, J. C. 1995. An empirical note on employed and unemployed job search. *Economics Letters*, 49 (4): 447–52.

Wall, H. J., and G. Zoega. 2002. The British Beveridge Curve: A tale of ten regions. *Oxford Bulletin of Economics and Statistics*, 64 (3): 257–76.

Wang, G., X. Wei, and J. Shen. 2005. Study on inter-provincial migration's influence on regional economic development in China [in Chinese]. *Fudan Journal* (Social Sciences Edition), 3: 148–61.

Wang, L. 2010. *Xian jieduan zhongguo shiye xianzhuang yuanyin ji duice fenxi* [Analysis on situations, reasons, and solutions of unemployment in modern China]. *Renli Ziyuan Guanli* [*Human Resource Management*], 2010: 220–221.

Wang, T., A. Maruyama, and M. Kikuchi. 2000. Rural-urban migration and labor markets in China: A case study in a northeastern province. *The Developing Economies*, 38 (1): 80–104.

Wang, X. 2008. *Woguo qiye shiyong jiuye zhongjie qingkuang tongji fenxi baogao* ["Survey on the use of job exchanges by enterprises in China]. In *Chinese Strategy Report 2007: Labor Market Intermediaries and Employment Promotion in China* [in Chinese], edited by X. Zeng. China Renmin University Press.

World Bank.1993. *New Skills for Economic Development: The Employment and Training implications of Urban Enterprise Reform.* Washington DC: World Bank.

Wu, J. 2005. *Understanding and Interpreting Chinese Economic Reform.* Mason, OH: Thomson/South-Western, 1st ed.

Wu, Z., and S. Yao. 2007. On unemployment inflow and outflow in urban China. *Regional Studies*, 40(8): 811-822.

Xiao, F. 2007, *Guoqi xinchou shikong yuanyu chanquan buming* [The loss of wage control in state-owned enterprises due to unclear property rights]. *Economic Herald*, 5: 84–84.

Xie, G. 2008. *Urban Labor Market in Transitional China: An Empirical Study on Layoff and Reemployment.* China: China Renmin University Press, 1st ed.

Xing, C. 2010. Migration, self-selection, and income distributions: Evidence from rural and urban China. *IZA Discussion Paper*, No. 4979.

Xinshengdai mingong yu mingonghuang [Generation of new rural migrants and shortage of migrant workers]. 2005. http://finance.sina.com.cn/nz / farmworker.

Xu, L. 2006. *Labor Market Segmentation in China: Towards an Analysis* [in Chinese]. Economic Science Press: 41–56.

Yan, Y. 2008. *Nongmingong: Gongxian, shouru fenpei yu jingji shehui fazhan* [Rural-urban migrant workers: Contribution, distribution, and development of the economy and society]. China Statistics Press: 44–9.

Yang, C. 2008. *Shiye Shuxing Yu Shiye Wenti Yanjiu* [A study of Unemployment Property and the Unemployment Problem in China]. China: Southwestern University Finance and Economics Press.

Zeng, X. 2008. Labor market intermediaries and employment promotion in China [in Chinese]. *Chinese Strategy Report 2007.* China Renmin University Press.

Zhao, R., and X. Li. 2005. *Woguo gongyi xing renli ziyuan zhongjie zuzhi de peiyu yu fazhan* [Development of public job exchanges in China]. *Inquiry into Economic Issues*, 8: 13–17.

Zhao, Y. 1999. Leaving the countryside: Rural-to-urban migration decisions in China. *The American Economic Review*, 89 (2): 281–6.

Zhao, Y. 2009. *Chengxiang Hexie Jiuye Lilun* [Harmonious Employment Theory of Urban and Rural Areas]. China: Jiangsu People's Press.

Zhao, Z. 2005. Migration, labor market flexibility, and wage determination in China: A review. *The Developing Economics*, 43 (2): 285–312.

Index